Postmodern Japanology Handbook

**Inter-Cultural Insights into Japanese
Pop Culture, Etymology of 日本語 &
Development of Language Education**

Isao Ebihara

GlobalEdAdvance
Press

Postmodern Japanology Handbook

Inter-Cultural Insights into Japanese Pop Culture, Etymology of 日本語 & Development of Language Education

Copyright © 2015 by Isao Ebihara

Library of Congress Control Number: 2015940953

Postmodern Japanology Handbook: Inter-Cultural Insights into Japanese Pop Culture, Etymology of ... & Development of Language Education

ISBN 978-1-935434-46-7

Ebihara, Isao 1956 -

Subject Codes and Description: 1: FOR014000 Foreign Language Study: Japanese   2: EDUCATION/Teaching Methods and materials/Language Arts: Japanese 3: SOC005000 Social Science: Customs and Traditions: Japanese

Cover design by Global Graphics

Printed in Australia, Brazil, France, Germany, Italy, Poland, Spain, UK, and USA and available on Espresso Book Machine.

Order books from www.gea-books.com/bookstore/
or any place good books are sold.

Published by
GlobalEdAdvancePRESS
a division of
Global Educational Advance, Inc.

DEDICATED TO

DONALD & CECILIA BODDEN

&

THE LATE JONATHAN TAKEO YOKOYAMA

(1929-2014)

TABLE OF CONTENTS

Postmodern Japanology Handbook

Inter-Cultural Insights into Japanese Pop Culture, Etymology of 日本語 & Development of Language Education

Publisher's Preface

Dr. Isao Ebihara, a native of Japan, has been teaching the Japanese language in the Vancouver area of B.C. since 2001. This book was written out of a realization that students need something more than a textbook. This work includes various levels of the Japanese language/culture to be utilized by students to review their learning and may also be a handbook for the Japanese culture as well as the language. It combines chapters of plain introduction of Japanese grammar and discussions of cultural components including culinary and pop culture together.

Postmodern Japanology Handbook is quite different from the author's previous three books: All the World is Anime; Shinto War Gods of Yasukuni Shrine; and Land of Rising Ghosts & Goblins. Not only does Dr. Ebihara combine language development with the Japanese culture, he ties it all together to bridge the gap for students looking for more than just a classroom educational experience. Dr. Ebihara's understanding of the dynamics of the early one room grammar school and current advanced Internet technology, are demonstrated in his language education process.

This book deals with various language education processes, such as economical, independent and collaborative learning. Dr. Ebihara builds on his bachelor and master's degrees in English literature in Japan, and master's level degrees in counseling in Canada, and a Doctor of Philosophy in the sociological integration of religion and society in the USA, to develop a handbook for language education. His experience in Japanese as well as western culture together with his education well qualifies him for teaching both Japanese and English language skills.

— **Hollis L. Green**, ThD, PhD, DLitt

INTRODUCTION

It took a little more than two years to complete this book, slightly longer than my third book "The Land of Rising Ghosts & Goblins." It was delayed due to several significant events my life. The largest event was my own marriage. On May 10, 2014, I married Beth Reba Bodden. From the time of engagement in October 2013, I didn't touched this project for nearly six months because it was pushed to the bottom of the priority list. Finally, I started the project again, approximately two weeks after the wedding.

I have been teaching the Japanese language to mostly college students in the Vancouver area of Canada since 2001. The majority of my students are Chinese and Korean, but some are westerners such as Canadians and Americans. During my teaching over the past 10 years, I came to realize that the syntax of the Japanese language is unique and significantly different from English and other European languages as well as other Asian tongues, for instance, the Chinese languages (or if you prefer, Cantonese or Mandarin). It also increased my awareness that the differences between syntaxes and writing systems of the Japanese and the ones of other languages give significant challenges to many students, particularly from the western hemispheres.

Due to such realization, I made a firm decision to write this book since I was convinced that students need something more than a textbook. Therefore, my intention to publish this book is for various levels of the Japanese language/culture learners to utilize it as a guidebook to review their learning. I also wanted to make this a guidebook for the Japanese culture as well as the language. I have also highlighted culinary and pop cultures because they have received the most attention worldwide in the previous few decades.

Thus, at the very start of this book, I want to clearly state that this is not a Japanese language textbook. Instead, this volume is a guidebook which combines chapters of plain introduction of Japanese grammar and discussions of cultural components including culinary and pop culture together. Some Japanese sample sentences for explaining grammar also introduce food and other items with cultural significance. I have paraphrased culturally significant cuisines, landmarks or anime/manga items, whenever readers are exposed to them in sample sentences.

The culinary and pop culture of the island nation has drawn a large amount of interest and fascination from students and other non-Japanese during the past several decades. At the end of this book, I bring a conclusion that might explain the raison d'etre of the Japanese language and culture, at least partially, rather than simply responding to a fascination in a trend or fad.

While I have been engaged in the writing project during the past two years, I have been hoping that this book might be able to give many students and other readers some new insights into the Japanese language that other text books could not provide.

Finally, I want to note that this book is dedicated to my inlaws Donald and Cecillia Bodden, and the late Jonathan Yokoyama (1932-2014). Yokoyama, my friend and mentor in Christian faith and language education over the past 10 years, who consistently endeavored to assist me in the understanding of Japanese Language education in Canada.

Part 1

Insights into Japanese Language and Education from Contemporary Culture

1

INTERNET,
JAPANESE LEARNING TECHNOLOGY,
YOUTUBE & POP CULTURE

Overview

Japanese language learners who started their studies after the *anime* and *manga* diaspora or the worldwide dispersion of these media are quite different from traditional language learners from the previous generation in many different ways. These new learners belong to the Otaku generation whose learning motives stem from the anime and manga world. They are fascinated by and deeply into the Medea, plots, stories and characters in the world that the authors created. The major goal and objective for these learners is the acquisition of the language in which anime and manga characters speak. Some of them are also inspired to make a living at producing anime and manga as authors or to find employment in these industries.

Otaku Generation & Japanese Language

There is an urgent need for schools around the planet that must be serious about developing Otaku friendly Internet based programs including language education. Governments around the world also must be aware of the need to modify the style of higher education and accommodates to the next generation with different learning style from the previous generation.

[1]The term Otaku (お宅) literally means "your or his home" and refers to someone who stays at home all the time and doesn't have a life outside of his or her fantasy world. This term was originally a derisive Japanese word used to refer to people with obsessive interests in the late 1980s. The term otaku refers to an overtly obsessive fan, or is specialized in any one particular theme, topic, or hobby. In modern Japanese slang, there are many subcategories of Otaku. Nevertheless, after the late 1990s, the term started to have more positive meanings which imply trendy, futuristic people with knowledge of pop culture and computer technology. The word was also exported into English language and became a part of universal vocabulary by the late 1990s.

Most commonly used subcategories are anime otaku (one who sometimes enjoys many days of excessive anime watching with no rest) and manga otaku (a fan of Japanese graphic novels), pasokon otaku (personal computer geeks), "gēmu" (game) otaku particularly anime and manga, as an Otaku generation of individuals who typically prefer living in their own realities or virtual castles similar to anime and manga world as princes or princesses in these personal universes. The virtual reality is the only comfort zone for an Otaku person, and he or she does not want interactions with people outside of his or her own reality. In the English speaking world, the term is used to refer to people who appear to be obsessed with Japan and its culture including anime otaku, manga otaku and gēmu (game) otaku. Also, the term did not contain negative implications from the very beginning of being part of English terminology.

Because of their unique lifestyle to prefer seclusion and privacy, some Otaku individuals also tend to study Japanese language alone without attending language classes in college and universities or privately funded language schools. They do so not for financial

---

1　　Isao Ebihara. All The World Is Anime. (Dayton, TN: USA: Global Ed Advance Press, 2010).

reasons or to live a frugal lifestyle, but they prefer independence, privacy and seclusion. Therefore, if an Otaku person decides to study Japanese or any other subjects, he or she wants to do it without interacting with teachers and classmates in the conventional reality. If such a person decides to have a teacher, he or she must choose a computer program as a teacher, so that he or she can learn the language systematically without interacting with another flesh and blood human. Such a person typically prefers machines or computer generated holographic persons as their friends to real people who reside in the real world, since he or she is afraid of the conventional realty in which non-virtual people live.

If Otaku people decide to come out of their own realities reluctantly and attend schools in our conventional reality, their best choice must be an Internet based e-educational schools without physical campuses. In such settings, students interact with human teachers with flesh and blood through computers, but not seeing each other in the same physical space. They will face anime characters which represent his teacher and all of his classmates. This kind of setting must be the most effective learning style for the Otaku generation learners since it makes them feel less intimidated to interact with other humans. Therefore, all colleges and universities must accommodate those in the younger generation with a totally different mentality and mindset from older ones.

YouTube & Online Learning Community

Otaku generation Japanese language learners utilize Internet media such as YouTube, Twitter and blogs. Many advanced learners create videos with their performances in Japanese and upload them to YouTube. These YouTube performers are a mixed population with both genders, both Otaku and non-Otaku, and various age groups. However, all of them are heavily into Japanese language and culture. Some of them managed to utilize these video presentations to promote their businesses and already earned the status as an Internet celebrity.

Also, beginners and young learners can also utilize these videos created by more advanced learners for their own learning. For example, some advanced learners teach the Te-form song and explains its grammar in the video, so that any newbies in Japanese can memorize the song. The number of YouTube Te-form Songs are increasing just like many other online language learning materials, and all of them are free. It is significant that YouTube and many other Internet media formulated Japanese learning communities in the past few years. The population of learners in these communities is growing and seemingly will continue to increase.

In online learning communities, members teach each other just like elementary school pupils who lived in rural communities of Tennessee in the earlier 20th century. Dr. Hollis L. Green (1933 -), the founder of Oxford Graduate School and Global Educational Advance, stated in his autobiographical book *So Tales* that his mother Grace Curton Green (1905 - 1996) was a grade school teacher who taught all of her pupils from grade one to eight simultaneously in a one room schoolhouse. It seems that there is some resemblance between today's online learning communities and the one room schoolhouses in the early 20th century, because in both settings people study economically, independently and collaboratively at the same time[2].

Hollis Green once asked his mother about the dynamics of the one room school. She answered that the fast learners were able to be challenged by listening to the upper class lessons, and the slow learners were able to review difficult lessons by hearing them taught to lower grades. Also, in a one room school a teacher would have to manage the class by having his or her students teach each other.

2   Hollis L. Green. *So Tales*. (Dayton, TN: USA: Global Ed Advance Press, 2012).

Usually, older and brighter students taught younger and less bright students. Each student also had a favorite and competent subject, and he or she could teach the subject to others. Green remarked that it was a challenge, but probably the best education that America has provided for the elementary and secondary levels.

In the online learning community, everyone is a student and a teacher and must teach each other just like young school boys in the 19th and early 20th centuries in rural North America without a sufficient number of teachers. In fact, a one room school which motivated students to study independently and collaboratively, was a much better learning system than today's school sytems in which there is much less flexibility and no chance for students to be involved in teaching one another. It seems that this is another repetition of a significant portion of the human history, since the one classroom school in a small village was a very economical and efficient educational system. People also longed for the economical and independent learning style that their ancestors had and brought back in the online community. It is completely understandable that those who were tired of "chicken pen" mass production style grade schools, high schools, colleges and universities seek for a refuge in Internet learning communities.

As it is said, "History repeats itself," i.e., significant events of human history recur many times. People also bring back past relics many times and utilize them if they are convenient and useful. For example, tablet style computers like Apple iPad or Samsung Galaxy with Android operating system are the reincarnation of stone-made slates that school boys and girls used during 19th and early 20th centuries. The stone slate remained as an archetype memory in people's collective unconscious. The electronic slate also replaced heavy textbooks made of paper.

Japanese TV Series on YouTube

BEGIN Japanology is a *NHK TV series* made for foreign tourists broadcasted from 2003, introducing numerous cultural topics of contemporary Japan including culinary and pop culture. It is created by many different authors, but the host of the program is Peter Barakan (1951 -   ), born in London with a degree in Japanese from the University of London. The topics included Ramen noodles, Nabe or Hot Pot Cuisine, Bento or lunch box, All You Can Eat in Tokyo, etc. The contents of this series are very informative and comprehensive, including both traditional and modern culture explaining how traditions evolved and the part they still play in people's everyday lives[3]. These videos are targeted to the students of Japanese culture as well as tourists and foreign residents in Japan. Many episodes from this series created after 2014 are viewable in YouTube.

Favorite Expressions for Japanese Language Learners

There is one impressive You Tube video in which several Japanese language learners who live in Japan and overseas introduce their own favorite expressions. Examples of these expressions are nouns or pronouns like "boku" (僕) or I (for men), "otenba" (お転婆) or Tomboy "yokai" (妖怪) or demon-like monster and "semi" (蝉), or cicada. Some other favorite expressions adjectives like "omoshiroi" (面白い) or interesting, "orokana" (愚かな) or foolish, "manpuku" (満腹) or full stomach, "tanoshii" (楽しい) or fun, and "aho" (あほ) or idiot. Other examples are phrases like "sorosoro shitsurei shimasu (そろそろ失礼します) or "It is time to leave", or "wakarimashita" (わかりました) "I understood". "Boku" is a first person singular pronoun for a male person only. However, the person who said that he likes this expression when a female uses it is because it makes her an attractive tomboy when she uses it. Likely this individual is an Otaku

---

3   BEGIN Japanology. http://beginjapanology.com.

who likes female characters who refer to themselves as "boku" in manga or anime movies.

Some foreigners like words like "yokai" and "semi" probably because "yokai" is a unique and distinct creature in Japanese mythology and folklore and cicadas are insects existing only in Asia. "Semi", or cicadas are fascinating for many visitors to Japan because they exist only in Asia and a limited area in North America. Some like the expression "ishin denshin" (以心伝心) or communicating without verbalizing. This is a unique statement which symbolizes higher context communication style with great emphasis on non-verbal communication such as eye contacts and facial expressions that I have discussed in the second chapter. Some of them report they like the word "henshin" (変身) which means "transform".

"Henshin" is very popular word among Otaku populations in Japan because many of the "Sentai" series and many other real time Japanese Sci-fi heroes transform into the fighting mode with formidable armor by screaming "Henshin". In the English speaking world, "Henshin" is generally translated into "morph," generally used in computer graphics and in the movie industry. The Japanese word was first translated into "morph" in 1992 when *Mighty Morphin Power Rangers* or the first English version of the Sentai series was created by Saban Entertainment and released in North America on TV. Although the term "morph" did not exist in the English speaking world before the introduction of the Power Rangers series, the word was quickly spread to the public. It became a popular word among all English speakers and is used outside of Sci-fi and Otaku world. The first Sentai series introduced to North America was "Kyoryu Sentai Jyuranger" (恐竜戦隊ジュウレンジャー) or "Dinosaur Taskforce Beast Rangers" created by the Toei Corporation. Saban Entertainment in USA modified the story setting and characters and released it as the first season of the Power Rangers series.[4] In the original "Jyuranger" story, the rangers were not humans but prehistoric "Saurian" or dinosaur type humanoid youngsters with much higher physical strength than humans and hibernated over millions of years.

All Sentai series created in Japan after the release of "Jyuranger" in 1992 were modified and introduced into North America and the rest of English speaking world as Power Rangers Series by Saban Entertainment. These rangers were sometimes modeled after race car drivers, police officers from outer space, fire fighters, pirates, samurais or ninjas. Many different kinds of Power Rangers over two decades created a worldwide "Rangers fad". Many of these who watched the Power Rangers series as children and teenagers, grew up as the first generation North American Otaku. These rangers will continue to emigrate to North America and other parts of the English speaking world as long as Japanese Toei continues to produce new rangers. There are also many knock offs and unofficial versions of Power Rangers like Ofunato's Sanma Rangers or Saury baking task force whose mission is to promote the consumption of fishery products of the local community.

The individuals who introduce their favorite Japanese expressions in the video presentations are a mixed bunch, but some are impressive and highly motivated individuals, strongly inspired to continue their Japanese language studies.

YouTube Videos Created by Japanese Language Learners

The next section highlights some of the YouTube creations that they have produced since 2010. Some of these individuals lived in Japan for many years, and others were new to Japan. Some also live outside of Japan but are committed to learning the language and culture. Many also create their videos as audio-visual resumes or part

---

4   However, in the English story that Saban created, these rangers were ordinary human teenagers who was attending a high school in LA.

of their online curriculur vitae that they can utilize for their career development and upload them to YouTube. These stories usually include personal histories of Japanese language learning; when, how and why they started studying this subject. They often include videos from a visit to Japan of people, homes, cities, bullet trains and food. The YouTube video presentations with such scenes often get immediate attention from viewers all over the world and receive many hits, since these items in a motion picture can be very exotic, strange and fascinating for viewers outside Japan.

Sammy grew up in Pennsylvania and studied Japanese in Hawaii before moving to Japan. She created both Japanese and English presentations. She also studied Korean when in the US. She had a job teaching English to young children and married a traditional Japanese chef who worked in an "Izakaya" (居酒屋) restaurant. Her favorite Japanese expression is a prefix "geki" (激) which intensifies adjectives and nouns. For instance "gekikara" (激辛) means extremely spicy and "gekiyasu" (激安) means an extremely low price.

One of her videos introduces typical Izakaya food that her husband serves and mentions that people also eat raw chicken that made her mother in Pennsylvania freak out[5]. Sammy introduces various snacks and "junk foods" sold in "konbini" or Japanese style convenience stores. She also introduced "natto" (納豆) or fermented soy bean for typical Japanese breakfast and "manjyu" (饅頭) traditional sweets made of soy beans and black beans in Tochigi prefecture. Also, Sammy showed YouTube that viewers suppon (鼈) or soft-shell turtle hotpot that her husband prepared for her. He was holding one live suppon and a sharp deba butcher knife at the beginning of the video. Viewers could see a delicious looking hotpot

---

5   Japan, China and some other Asian countries developed agricultural farms in which farmers breed chickens and other farm animals in a germ free environment. It is considered completely safe to consume chickens or pork bred in such farms without heating.

dinner with suppon meat, eggs and vegetables that Sammy and her husband were ready to eat. After the meal, Sammy said "arigato" (有難う) or "Thank you" to the suppon whom her husband slaughtered for meal. In her video there was no gruesome or gory scene of decapitation and butchering of the creature like those of some Japanese national YouTubers. Since her husband is a chef making traditional Japanese food, the majority of her presentations are predominantly foodie videos.

Hannah Minx is another YouTub producer who has created numerous presentations about Japanese language and culture. She introduced at least one Japanese expression or one feature of Japanese life in each video she created. In the summer of 2012, she was the most prolific author among YouTubers who created videos about Japanese language and culture. Most of her videos were designed to introduce simple Japanese expressions to those in the English speaking world. Minx is based in the US instead of Japan and usually stays there. She was still attending school there when she started her YouTube video series. Minx looks like a typical Otaku girl who dresses up like an anime character and wears rabbit ears on her head. Her appearance also has a close resemblance to "Elvira" an American real time movie character because of her long, dark hair. Minx compares herself with Elvira a few times in her videos. She also has a business to sell her own specialty products named "Minxy" and utilized the YouTube videos to market her own products. She was also interviewed by Converge, a US TV program targeting youth and young adult viewers[6]. In the Converge interview, she revealed that Minx is a pseudonym. Minxy products created under her pseudonym are mostly cute and trendy accessory items of Japanese origin.

Hannah seems extremely bright, attractive, ambitious and entrepreneurial, a person who utilized her Japanese language skills to

---

6   The Converge interview on Hannah Minx is also on YouTube.

build her fame and business. Minx is also an extremely inspirational person and seemingly has already obtained the status of global Internet celebrity among Otaku and others of the Internet population. She often applies kanji "hana" (花) which means flower to her name and writes her name "hana minkusu" (花ミンクス) in Japanese. She was also one of the participants in the video in which foreigners in Japan introduced favorite Japanese words, and her favorite expressions are "utsu" (鬱) or depression and "wagamama" (わがまま) or selfish.

　　Minx named a series of videos introducing short Japanese expressions, JWOW which is the acronym "Japanese Word Of The Week". She was uploading these videos weekly and some examples of expressions that she introduced in her videos were "soji suru" (掃除する) or cleaning your property, and "mushi-atsui" (蒸し暑い) which means "muggy" or "hot and humid". She introduced "inu" (犬) or dog and "neko" (猫) or cat showing a real dog and stuffed cat in her video. Another example of JWOW videos Minx uploaded was one in which she introduced the expression "undo suru" (運動する) which means, "Do physical exercises". She demonstrated a push up action and did it ten times while counting from one to ten in Japanese like "ichi" 1, "ni" 2, "san" 3, "yon" 4, "go" 5, "roku" 6, "nana" 7, "hachi" 8, "kyuu" 9 and "jyuu" 10. The JWOW series were very brief and memorable for viewers for using real-time objects and her own actions in the presentations.

　　Minx has another series titled "Miss Hannah Minx Japanese Lessons" which covers several idiomatic expressions like "saiko" (最高) or "excellent", and "honto ni" (本当に) or "really". Besides JWOW and Miss Hannah Minx Japanese Lessons series, Minx produced videos to introduce various features of Japanese culture. She discussed the topic of typical Asian non-verbal communications using gestures in video and emoticon or text to express emotions with subtitles. Minx also created some foodie videos with topics such as "Eating raw food", and "Soba noodles". Minx videos are successful in appealing to the Otaku generation since they are animated, visual, plain and clear, and also inherently carry the author's philosophical assumptions and intentionality.

Japanese Pop Culture & Vocaloid

I am going to introduce another product named Vocaloid that Japanese Pop Culture and computer technology created and Otaku generation Japanese learners are keen on as well as Japanese nationals. [7]The most well known Vocaloid character is Hatsune Miku (初音ミク), a singing synthesizer application with a female persona, developed by Crypton Future Media. As stated in the previous chapter, there is a version of Te-form Song with a different tune from Battle Hymn of the Republic in the YouTube sung by Miku. The name of the character comes from a fusion of the Japanese for first初 (hatsu), sound音 (ne) and future未来 or ミク (Miku). The combination of two Kanji 未来, normally reads as "mirai", however it is pronounced "Miku" in this case. With the Vocaloid program, users are able create a music video in which Hatsune Miku and other Vocaloid characters sing any song in any tune and language. Soon after the release of the Miku program on August 31, 2007, users of Nico Nico Douga, a Japanese website similar to YouTube, started posting videos with songs created using her sound bank. The Hatsune Miku character was originally Maker Hikōshiki Hatsune Mix, the protagonist of a manga written by Kei Garō. The story by Garō explores the many possibilities of story-telling and has featured numerous adventures of Miku, ranging from giant-sized battles with Hatsune Miku to home exploits. Nevertheless, there is no single storyline and the entire setting within the narrative is unofficial. Miku is also the protagonist of a various non-commercial fanfiction type manga series posted on the Internet, and numerous

---

7   Wikipedia: Hatsune Miku. Ibid.

parodies of the Miku character have come into existence as well. In the English speaking world, the Vocaloid software has also had a great influence on the character Black Rock Shooter, who looks like Hatsune Miku but is not linked to her by design[8].

Facebook in Japan

Facebook[9], an online social networking service with global popularity has also permeated the Japanese population[10]. Matt Lundy (2012) maintained that Facebook was a fringe player in Japan's social networking culture in the past. He contends that according to statistics from Socialbakers analysis, about 2% of Japan's online population was registered on Facebook in 2011, compared with roughly 60% in the United States. However, Japanese Facebook population quickly grew after that, and grew by 10 times by 2012[11].

Lundy contends that Japanese people typically esteem privacy and do not reveal their real names on the web, instead opting for pseudonyms that allow them to freely express themselves without fear of reproach. However, after several years of growing pains, Facebook is finally gaining approval in the Far East, suggesting that online behaviour in Japan is shifting toward a Zuckerbergian[12] culture of sharing, transparency and personal connection.

Lundy contends, "In the last year alone, Facebook membership has more than tripled, including a flood of 2.6 million new users in

---

8   Wikipedia: Hatsune Miku. Ibid.
9   Facebook (formerly [thefacebook]) is an online social networking service launched on February 4, 2004. After registering to the site, users may add a user profile, and other users as "friends". Users can exchange messages, post status updates and photos, share videos and receive notifications when others update their profiles.
10   Wikipedia: http://en.wikipedia.org/wiki/Facebook
11   Matt Lundy. Facebook and Japan finally friend each other: Canadian Business. http://www.canadianbusiness.com/blogs-and-comment/facebook-and-japan-finally-friend-each-other/
12   Wikipedia: Mark Elliot Zuckerberg. Online at http://en.wikipedia.org/wiki/Mark_Zuckerberg

the final half of 2011. Last month's comScore report showed that Facebook pulled ahead of Mixi in monthly unique visitors, second only to Twitter, though Japanese people are spending twice as long on their Facebook accounts as they are tweeting".

Lundy also maintains that another reason for Facebook's final approval on Japanese soil is that users there are realizing that some modicum of anonymity is still possible on the site. It is not uncommon for Japanese Facebook users to shield their identities through false profile photos or usernames.

Netouyo & Other Antisocial Net Users

"Neotouyo" is an abbreviation for "Net Uyoku". Uyoku means right-wing in Japanese. Therefore, Netouyo is antisocial Japanese ultra-nationalists (or racists) who use the internet to spread their vile propaganda "Koreans are the slowest people in the world" or "Chinese are evil." They are as counter-productive as more traditional やくざ 右翼 "Yakuza Uyoku" or 任侠右翼 "Ninkyo Uyoku", equally causing troubles to the public[13].

However, these two have several critical differences. While traditional Yakuza Uyoku is physically violent and associated with Yakuza syndicates, Netouyo does not have links with such criminal organizations. They demonstrate no violent conduct in the physical world, while they practice antisocial activities on the Internet. They simply use the internet and post extremely narrow-minded and annoying statements to blogs and news articles. In a sense, they are a "subspecies" of traditional Otaku, in a narrower sense, prior to the 1990s. They stay at home all the time and don't have a social life, or love life. Basically, they pass the time by watching anime, playing videogames and surfing the internet[14].

---

13 Isao Ebihara. *Shinto War Gods of Yasukuni Shrine*. (Dayton, TN: USA: Global Ed Advance Press, 2011)

14 Isao Ebihara. *All The World IS Anime*. Ibid.

[15] Vocaloid: Hatsune Miku Photo [16].

_____

15 Was available September 2012: www.fanpop.com
16 The picture is used under "fair dealing" (Canada) and "fair use" (USA) provisions in copyright law.

NOTES

2

SHINTO, BUDDHIST MOTIFS & SPIRITUALITY IN THE OTAKU WORLD

It is generally agreed that Shinto and Buddhist motifs and worldviews passed on from the Asuka Period (538-710) are still very influential in today's Japanese society and lifestyle. For instance, Toshi Densetsu or Japanese urban legends, in which preternatural creatures attack ordinary people, are based on Shinto and Buddhist motifs. The motifs of 怨霊 (onryo), Japanese ghosts who have become vengeful spirits and take their aggression out on any and all who cross their path instead of just fantastical and animistic 妖怪 (yokai) or supernatural creatures of earlier Japanese folklore and myth, stem from either Shinto or Buddhist myth.

Shinto & Buddhist Motifs

The first Shinto premise is that some individuals with remarkable achievements change into Kami (神) or a Shinto deity at the end of their lives. The second premise is that the souls of the dead are expected to go to a dark afterlife, the Land of Yomi. According to Kojiki, the oldest written literature in Japan, a compilation of pre-historic myths and legends, the afterlife is similar to the Greek concept of Hades in which all were destined to go regardless of their conduct during their lifetime. However, the second premise faded out among Japanese population after the introduction of Buddhism, since the idea of Yomi or Hades was obviously not a comfort for most Japanese[17].

Buddhism also has two different and apparently contradictory concepts about the afterlife. One is reincarnation or "transmigration of souls," the most well-known afterlife concept of Buddhism. In this, there is neither heaven nor hell. The dead simply have a rebirth after death either as a human or animal, depending on their conduct during their life. If a person had virtuous and honorable conduct throughout their entire life, he or she will be reincarnated into a family with more wealth and higher prestige. In the ideal scenario, this person might even be an emperor or empress. On the other hand, if a person has poor behavior and a dishonorable lifestyle, he or she will be born into the next life in poverty and a lower socioeconomic status. In the worst scenario, this person may be an animal and consumed as food by some other human or by animals.

The second well known afterlife concept of Buddhism is a migration to the Pure Land or the celestial realm which belongs to Buddha or Bodhisattva (minor Buddha). Pure Land is a Buddhist heaven in which only those with good conduct and character are allowed to enter. The Mahāyāna Buddhists who believe in Pure Land also believe in the hell ruled by Yama or Enma Dai-Ō (閻魔大王), the ruler of Hades, the destination of those whose conduct is not honorable during their lifetime.

The concept of Pure Land was the product of the influence of Christianity introduced to India by the Apostle Thomas, since the original Buddhism introduced by Gautama Buddha did not include it. The goal and objective of the original Buddhism is "nirvana" or the extinction of desire and individual consciousness instead of transmigration to the Buddhist heaven. They simply pursued the

17 Isao Ebihara. *Land of Rising Ghosts & Goblins*. (Dayton, TN: USA: Global Ed Advance Press, 2012)

nothingness or annihilation of existence, since reincarnation or repetition of the same boring life was curse for them. The original teaching of Gautama Buddha was passed on to his disciples, but was not understood by a larger population. The teaching which viewed the nothingness or annihilation of self was the ultimate enlightenment and peace was incomprehensible for the majority of Indians. Then, so-called Pure Land schools took over the main stream of Buddhism after Thomas introduced the Gospel to India. The new schools of Buddhism became so popular not only in India, but also China, so that they were eventually introduced to Japan.

The Mahāyāna Buddhist was the most popular and predominant among Pure Land schools. It believes that if a person migrates into the Pure Land once, he or she stays there forever, never dies and becomes another human or animal. The migration to the Pure Land or the celestial realm which belongs to Buddha or Bodhisattva (minor Buddha) is an extremely well known afterlife concept of Buddhism besides reincarnation.

On the other hand, there is no unanimous view about whether people may exit from the Buddhist hell or not. Some believe that hell is a final and ultimate destiny for sinners with eternal torture and gnashing pain. If someone goes to the hell once, the process is completely irreversible and there is no way to exit from there, similar to the orthodox Christian belief. Others believe that if a person spends a certain length of time there, he or she may be able to leave. However, one must spend millions or billions of years of torment, and he or she must start a new life from the lowest form of existence such as an insect or a worm.

Japanese also have a belief in Kekkai (結界), or a spiritual barrier or force field which prevents Yōkai (妖怪) and Oni (鬼) from entering their territory. They believe that their country is protected by this spiritual boundary from foreign thoughts, religions and spirituality which might challenge and undermine their traditional way of thinking, national identity or "Japaneseness."

Preternatural Creatures in Japanese Mythology

In my third book, *Land of Rising Ghosts & Goblins* (2012) [18], I have discussed the motifs of supernatural creatures of earlier Japanese folklore and myth which include the fantastical and animistic Yōkai (妖怪), onryo (怨霊), Japanese ghosts who have become vengeful spirits stemmed from either Shinto or Buddhist myths. It is fascinating that these motifs of supernatural creatures are impacting today's Otaku and Japanese pop culture as well as traditional literatures and high culture originating in this archipelago.

In my previous publications, I have introduced *My Neighbor Totoro* (1988) [19], *Princess Mononoke* (1997)[20] *Spirited Away* (2001)[21] written by Hayao Miyazaki (1941 -   )[22] as examples that indicate that Shinto based animism is strongly impacting today's anime and Otaku culture. In his work, Miyazaki conveys positive, timely and sociologically relevant messages that support environmental conservation and are expressed through pagan spirituality and Shinto ideals of respect for nature.

Many Shinto sects are linked with Japanese ultra-nationalist and Pre-Second World War totalitarian ideology that "Netouyo" and "Yakuza Uyoku" follow and have also influenced some of today's anime and manga artists. However, Miyazaki is a practitioner of primitive folk Shinto instead of modern age State Shinto with a strong linkage to Japanese nationalism ideology or pre-Second World War militarism. He is rather critical to the Pre-Second World

18 Isao Ebihara. *Land of Rising Ghosts & Goblins*. Ibid.
19 Wikepedia: http://en.wikipedia.org/wiki/My_neighbor_totoro
20 Wikepedia: Princess Mononoke. Was available March 2011: http://en.wikipedia.org/wiki/Princess_mononoke
21 Wikipedia.org/wiki/Spirited_Away
22 Wikepedia: Hayao Miyazaki. Was available March 2011: http://en.wikipedia.org/wiki/Hayao_Miyazaki

War totalitarian Imperial Japan led by the non-democratic military government, viewing them as nothing more than the oppressors of humanity. Thus, most of Miyazaki's manga and anime work convey a primitive Shinto perspective that is similar to worldwide Western and non-Western animism through characters and themes. In his work, Shinto based spiritual creatures are often antagonistic to humanity, but not fundamentally evil or destructive like onryo (怨霊) or vengeful spirits.

However, many anime and manga stories describe the world of more harmful, distractive and vengeful spirits. Besides Miyazaki's work, I have introduced InuYasha (犬夜叉)[23], a Feudal Fairy Tale or Sengoku Otogizōshi (戦国御伽草子) written by Japanese anime and manga series by Rumiko Takahashi(1957 -)[24], and *GeGeGe no Kitaro* (ゲゲゲの鬼太郎)[25] by Shigeru Mizuki (1922 -)[26], a couple of masterpieces written by popular anime and manga masters in Japan. Both masterpieces describe the world of animistic Yōkai (妖怪) and onryo (怨霊), or human ghosts who have become vengeful spirits. Both narratives clearly indicate that the supernatural creatures of earlier Japanese folklore and myth stemmed from either Shinto or Buddhist myth are still dominating the world of anime and manga.

Soul Reapers in Bleach

Bleach (2006)[27], written by Tite Kubo (1977 -   )[28] is one of the contemporary anime and manga products that stems from Buddhist mythology and spirituality describing distractive and vengeful spirits. The protagonist of *Bleach* is Ichigo Kurosaki, a teenager in Karakura

---

23   Wikepedia: InuYasha. http://en.wikipedia.org/wiki/InuYasha
24   Wikepedia: Rumiko Takahashi. http://en.wikipedia.org/wiki/Rumiko_ Takahashi
25   Wikepedia: GeGeGe no Kitaro. http://en.wikipedia.org/wiki/GeGeGe_no_ Kitaro
26   Wikepedia: Shigeru Mizuki. http://en.wikipedia.org/wiki/Shigeru_Mizuki
27   Wikipedia.org/wiki/Bleach_(manga)
28   Wikipedia.org/wiki/Tite_Kubo

Town who is gifted with the ability to see spiritual entities. Ichigo's life is drastically changed by the sudden appearance of a girl named Rukia Kuchiki who is a Soul Reaper—one of many entrusted with the preservation of the flow of souls between the World of the Living and the dead.

After Rukia is badly injured by the battle with "Hollows" or an evil spiritual entity, Ichigo gets involved in the preternatural world as a substitute Soul Reaper to replace her temporarily. Rukia obtains a temporary body and assists Ichigo as a human after losing power as a Soul Reaper. The world of the dead is called Soul Society which is loosely modelled after the afterlife imagery of Pureland Buddhism. However, the society is very earthly and hiarchical and resembles feudal Japan during the Medeaval Era rather than Buddhism heaven. They live under the rulership with dictatorial power, and the "Soul King" is an enigmatic being who resides in an extremely well protected space in a different dimention from the rest of the Soul Society.

People who live there are immortal spiritual beings without physical bodies and supposed to live forever unless they are destroyed by enemies. When a resident of the Soul Society dies, he or she is reincarnated into a human baby of the world of the living, having eliminated the entire memory of the previous life.

The missions of Soul Reapers are two-fold. First, they are directing the souls of the dead to the Soul Society safely. Chances are high that the dead might become [29]Hollows or dangerous and vengeful lost souls like "onryo" in traditional mythology if they stay in the world of the living for too long. Second, Soul Reapers must destroy the Hollows who are exercising supernatural power and harming the living. Rukia and other Soul Reapers do not possess physical bodies because they are spiritual beings who belong to the supernatural world. However, they are able to use temporary bodies while they do

---

29   Hollows are evil spirits evolved from human ghosts.

their work in the world of the living. A temporary body may be either a living or dead human or animal body or even inanimate thing such as a stuffed animal.

Just like any human society on earth, the Soul Society has many conflicts, conspiracies, and dissensions within. Rukia was captured by her superior Soul Reaper and transfered back to the the Soul Society and sentenced to death for the illegal act of transfering her powers into Ichigo who was a living human. Ichigo rescued her with the aid of several of his spiritually aware classmates like Uryū, Orihime Inoue and Yasutora "Chad" Sado and a fraction of Soul Reapers. After having several battles with antagonistic fractions in the Soul Society, Ichigo obtains the power, which exceeds captain-level soul reapers and recognition as allies with his friends of the Soul Society. In order to defeat Aizen, the most powerful dissenter of the Soul Society, Ichigo undergoes intense training with his father Isshin, revealed to be a former Soul Reaper, and becomes an equal to his archenemy. Finally, Ichigo defeated Aizen and imprisoned him, but lost power as a Soul Reaper becoming a normal human as a side effect of the final blow on Aizen. However, 17 months later, Ichigo regains his Soul Reaper powers after encountering a group of humans possessing super-natural powers. The battle of Ichigo as a Soul Reaper continues. [30]The Soul Reaper in Bleach anime and manga might have a close parallel with The Soul Collector from a 1999 television movie in the USA[31].

Zachariah, a young and inexperienced Soul Collector makes a few mistakes and Mordecai his supervisor decided that he is to live as a human for 30 days. Then, Zachariah falls in love with the ranch owner, Rebecca, a widowed single mother who recently lost her husband. The Soul Reapers and Soul Collectors do similar jobs based on comparable story settings in which preternatural beings from the spiritual world collect souls of the dead and transport them to the

30   US TV Movie, 1999.
31   http://en.wikipedia.org/wiki/The_Soul_Collector

afterlife. However, the philosophical assumptions of these two stories are fundamentally different, since "The Soul Collector" is based on the Christian afterlife belief system, while "Bleach" is based on the secular and loosely Buddhist worldview. The collectors were beings from the divine kingdom ruled by one and only God instead of carnal and earthly "Soul Society" which resembles the human kingdom.

The difference between the two story settings might indicate eloquently that the average Japanese views the afterlife as an extension of the earthly life if they believe in it. It is worldly and carnal and there is nothing sacred in it. In funeral events, many Japanese place very substantial amounts of money in the coffin, believing that the dead might need money in the next life. Therefore, it is easy to conclude that the story setting of Bleach is a reflection of the typical Japanese afterlife concept.

[32]Bleach Photo[33]

_____

32   www.azhime.com

33   The picture is used under "fair dealing" (Canada) and "fair use" (USA) provisions in copyright law.

3

LANGUAGE TO CONCEAL & REVEAL

(Higher Context Nature of Parable & "Keigo"敬語 or Super-polite expressions)

General Overview & Parables in the New Testament

It is generally believed that Asian cultures and languages are higher-context than the Western cultures. In a lower-context society, almost all statements are more literal and generally crystal clear to everyone. However, in a higher-context society, there are many ambiguous statements that only insiders can understand. Japanese and many Asian cultures are considered higher context than almost all Western, particularly North American cultures, and therefore language learners find it difficult to decode some expressions.

Higher-context language is similar to the parables that Jesus Christ used in the New Testament. The parable is a mode of communication with extensive use of stories and allegorical and figurative expressions instead of directly telling the students or audience. It was a form of communication that only those who belong to certain ethnic or faith groups were able to comprehend. In the context of the New Testament, the parable is comprehensible only for those who are open to his teaching and ready to accept it. Jesus once stated that the parable has a dual function to both conceal and reveal. It conceals the truth from those who are stubborn and not ready to accept it, but reveals it to those who earnestly pursue it.

Higher-Context Communications in the Non-Western World

The higher-context communications are not exclusive to the non-Western world. There are many idioms, allegorical and figurative expressions in the English speaking world. For instance, the expression, "Running around like a chicken with its head chopped off" might not be comprehensible for those who are new in the English speaking world. It is a figurative expression to describe busyness and restlessness of a person. It is a symbolic expression that the person is "brainless". However, if this person is literally "brainless" or "headless", he or she is instantaneously dead, so it is obviously not to be taken literally.

Although this expression is idiomatic and allegorical, it is more universal and easier to comprehend particularly for those from agrarian communities than most Japanese idioms.

A similar Japanese idiom has a completely different meaning. The Suppon or softshell turtles' head remains active for half an hour after the moment of decapitation because the reptiles have a slower metabolism than mammals or avian.

Therefore the Suppon is regarded as a symbol of persistence because it does not release the object once it bites a certain object even after the head is removed from the body. They say: Kaminari ga naru made hanasanai (雷がなるまで放さない) or "(Suppon) does not release anything until the thunder strikes". The suppon's decapitated head may win the chef's finger tip in exchange for its life[34].

---

34   Some Japanese authors maintain that one may understand the true meaning of the customary meal time expression いただきます (itadakimasu) when he or she observes the gruesome decapitation of Suppon. In Chapter 7, I noted that it was originally a full sentence, 命をいただきます (inochi o itadakimasu) which means "I will take your life".

Japanese also made a different idiom, Tsuki to Suppon (月と すっぽん) or Moon and Soft-shell turtle to symbolize two items that look similar but with completely different natures. The soft-shell turtle is round like the moon as its hot-pot dish is called Maru-nabe (丸鍋) or "round hot-pot". However the creature is ugly in contrast with the beautiful full moon. Unless they consumed the meat, people would not see the creature because it mostly stays in water. For the Japanese gourmet population, this idiom might mean that two round items have completely different aesthetic values, since the moon is beautiful but not edible. On the other hand, the soft-shell turtle has been known for the exquisite taste in the Asian region from the antiquity despite its grotesque appearance. Both idioms concerning the soft-shell are comprehensible only among the population with the custom of meat consumption of the soft-shell.

In higher context societies like Japan and the Middle East, East and South Asia, there are many factors other than idioms to block outsiders to comprehend their expressions. In these cultures, there is an overwhelming number of nonverbal factors like tone of voice, facial expressions, and eye contact. These nonverbal factors are vital in courtship and various relationships in these societies over millennia. There have been many verbal, nonverbal and symbolic interactions between masters and servants, husband and wife, parents and children. They are also very hierarchical and the socially inferior ones are expected to use humble and polite ways of communication both verbally and nonverbally in front of a superior one.

[35]Edward T. Hall (1914 - 2009) is a respected anthropologist and cross-cultural researcher who identified the concepts of higher-context and lower-context in the 1960's. This was used to categorize differences in communication styles. [36]According to Hall, higher-

35   Wikepedia: Edward T. Hall. Online at http://en.wikipedia.org/wiki/Edward_T._ Hall
36   Edward T. Hall. Beyond Culture. (New York: Anchor Press/Doubleday, 1976)

context cultures require extra tools or "decrypters" for decoding communications. He states that higher-context transactions feature pre-programmed information that was in the receiver and in the setting, with only minimal information in the transmitted message. Lower-context transactions were the reverse and most of the information must be in the transmitted message in order to make up for what is missing in the context. Meaning of the language was more literal and there was little room for ambiguity or multiple messages of the same statement.

According to Hall, Japanese and most other East Asian societies were generally considered higher-context than the US and Canada and most other Western countries, and communications therefore required an extra tool of decoding. One could compare this to the communication styles of men and women in which women often place more unspoken meaning in their words. This could be considered more higher-context than men who are more literal.

Higher-Context Culture & Homogeneity

[37]Rieko Maruta Richardson, Sandi W. Smith (2007) wrote an intriguing paper which contrasted Japanese and American society by observing Hall's theory of higher and lower- context societies. Richardson and Smith maintain that in a lower-context culture is generally a society with greater cultural diversity and heterogeneity. In such a society, verbal skills are more necessary and, therefore, "more highly prized". In terms of communication, very little is taken for granted or to be understood without verbal explanation. In other words, a heterogonous society cannot afford to have "secret codes" that only group members comprehend, since it is a collection of many different groups.

37 Rieko Maruta Richardson and Sandi W. Smith. The influence of high/low-context culture and power distance on choice of communication media: Students' media choice to communicate with Professors in Japan and America. International Journal of Intercultural Relations 31, 2007 p. 479–501

In a higher-context culture however, according to Richardson and Smith, "cultural homogeneity encourages suspicion of verbal skills, confidence in the unspoken, and eagerness to avoid confrontation". In general, higher-context communication employ indirect verbal expression and implication embedded in nonverbal communication.

According to their observation, cultural homogeneity of Japanese society is the crucial factor to make the nation higher-context. Japan has been a homogenous society at least over millennia or during the most part of written history. Since the nation has been a homogenous and exclusive society for such a long time, she has developed many in-group expressions that only insiders could comprehend.

[38]Also, during the Edo Period (1603 - 1868), Japan had two centuries of national seclusion from 1639 to 1854 in order to keep the nation away from Western and Christian influence. Shogun Tokugawa Iemitsu (1604 — 1651)[39] enacted the foreign relations policy named Sakoku (鎖国) meaning "locked country" around the time of the Shimabara Rebellion. Under Sakoku no foreigner could enter or any Japanese leave the country on penalty of death. After the policy was enacted, the government closed all ports in the country and terminated diplomatic relationships with most Western nations after expelling the missionaries. The Sakoku policy continued until US Commodore Matthew Perry (1794-1858)[40] visited Uraga Harbor near Edo (modern Tokyo) and demanded that Japan open its doors to the world. Because of the long period of seclusion, the nation became highly homogenous. The homogeneity went to the level of animal species in the Galápagos Islands and the Japanese population became culturally and genetically isolated and thus a high-context communication style.

---

38 Isao Ebihara. *Land of Rising Ghosts & Goblins*. (Dayton, TN: USA: Global Ed Advance Press, 2012)

39 Wikipedia: Tokugawa Iemitsu. http://en.wikipedia.org/wiki/Tokugawa_Iemitsu

40 Wikipedia: Matthew Perry. http://en.wikipedia.org/wiki/Matthew_C._Perry

After the Meiji Restoration in 1868, the Tokugawa shogunate government was defeated and the Japanese nation was rapidly westernized and modernized. The nation's communication style became slightly lower-context, since the new government vigorously introduced western culture to the general public. However, the nation remained higher-context in comparison with Western nations and even other Asian nations like China. The authoritarian and totalistic Meiji government wanted the nation to continue to be homogeneous and hold the Confucianism mentality to honor elders and the leadership. In fact, the Meiji Government invented *Kokutai* (国体, lit. national essence/entity/polity)[41], an ideological system and "moral concept that constituted the very essence of the state" around the emperor system. It was the ideological system based on the supreme authority of the emperor as the inviolable high priest or spiritual head of the nation. In this ideological system, the entire state was a unitary sacro-society or form of cultic religious community that involved the emperor, government and all citizens or subjects of the country[42]. Besides respecting the nation's leadership the totalitarian Meiji government forced people to regard the emperor as a god and to blind submission to the regime[43].

Lafcadio Hearn[44] lived in the 19th century and did an in-depth study of Japanese culture, spirituality and the world of "yokai[45]" or Japanese demon like monsters and ghosts after immigrating to Japan from Britain under the Meiji government. He wrote many short stories dealing with paranormal activities throughout Japanese history and

41 Wikipedia: Kokutai. Online at http://en.wikipedia.org/wiki/Kokutai
42 Ebihara. Shinto War Gods of Yasukuni Shrine. ibid.
43 Isao Ebihara. Land of Rising Ghosts & Goblins. (Dayton, TN: USA: Global Ed Advance Press, 2012)
44 Wikipedia: Lafcadio Hearn. Online at http://en.wikipedia.org/wiki/Lafcadio_Hearn
45 Wikipedia: Yōkai. Online at http://en.wikipedia.org/wiki/Y%C5%8Dkai

compiled them in a book titled Kwaidan[46]. One of the stories deals with "Noppera-bō" (のっぺら坊) or faceless ghost. Many scholars and critics in later years argued that Hearn's "Noppera-bō" might imply Japanese society under the Meiji government. These critics debated if he was referring to Noppera-bō as a symbol of Japanese society that was westernized and modernized only from the outside and was covertly criticizing the Meiji government. That is, Japanese society was modernized externally but was completely foreign to the concept of democracy and was Noppera-bō or faceless. This facelessness continued until the nation's final defeat in the Second World War which took place in the summer of 1945.

After the Second World War, Western style democracy was introduced to Japan for the first time. Twice as many loan words came into the Japanese language from the English speaking world than the Meiji Period (1868 - 1912). The communication style of the general public shifted slightly to the side of lower-context after the war, since the nation adapted to American style communication. However, the nation still held to the higher-context tradition as well as the hierarchical social life and did not abandon numerous nonverbal expressions at work and home. For example, in Japanese corporations and government offices, junior members use both hands to hold cups when they receive sake from their bosses. On the other hand, bosses need only one hand when they receive the drink from their subordinate.

However, a real change happened in the new millennium or the dawning era of globalization. Now all nation-states and local communities can no longer remain homogenous and are forced to accept new immigrants. Many business corporations in Japan were forced to become heterogeneous and hire employees from the USA and many Asian and European countries. In the new era many large

---

46   Lafcadio Hearn. Kwaidan. (North Clarendon, VT: USA: Tuttle Publishing, 1904/1971)

Japanese companies were successfully globalized and no longer Japanese in a traditional sense. Therefore, the leadership in these corporations had to employ a lower-context and immigrant friendly communication style. Smaller companies will follow the footsteps of larger companies and transform sometime in the near future. Soon, all boundaries between nation-states will be demolished and the communication style of the people in Japan will continue to change.

On the other hand, the United States and Canada have been heterogeneous from the beginning since it has been a melting pot of all kinds of immigrants. A heterogeneous society like those in North America cannot afford to develop secret, nonverbal expressions that only a small group of people can understand. In the US, the leadership worked hard to maintain the unity and coherency of the society from the day that the nation declared independence. Therefore the use of clear and plain English that everyone understands cannot be overemphasized.

Higher-Context Culture in Japanese Imperial Court

Among Japanese society, the court-culture of the imperial family and its surroundings was much more higher-context or culturally encrypted and therefore decoding the communications was extremely difficult even for the average Japanese person. For anyone who was not well versed with the culture of the imperial court, what the emperor and his family members spoke made no sense at all. Japanese court has been such an exclusive and homogenous society that no outsiders were allowed to join for nearly two millennia. The imperial family practiced inter-marriage and became inbred within a small group during an extremely long period. The family developed numerous physical and mental disabilities among its members. The imperial family developed extremely higher context court culture, since it has been a secret society nearly 2000 years. The court has a distinct language with its own unique vocabulary that only insiders can understand.

Also, this outstanding higher-context and aristocratic court language was an effective tool of survival, and sometimes deception, for Japan's emperors throughout the long period that the emperors' powers were marginalized, remained dormant or were almost invisible for centuries. The Fujiwara Clan took the real political power around the 7th Century, then in the late 12th century, by the hands of Shogun or the Samurai-class second monarchy. Since the state of the emperors' dormancy or invisibility continued until the Meiji Restoration in 1868, Hirohito's ancestors were forced to develop some drastic means for survival. They developed a covert, subtle and encrypted court language to protect themselves from politically more powerful rulers or second monarchies.

The only power that the emperor possessed during the long period of "imperial dormancy[47]", was to manipulate rulers and warlords by giving out official titles or awards to them that they always craved. For minor warlords, receiving titles higher than they deserved was quite dangerous because it provoked the jealousy of others. The emperor sometimes gave people whom he didn't like higher titles than they deserved in order to destroy them. Throughout the centuries the emperor was a clever fox or snake who could easily slay lions and tigers without using his claws.

For instance, Emperor Goshirakawa (1127-1192) of Medieval Japan era, was one of best examples of emperors who lived like a fox or serpent, exercising the exquisite skills of deceptions. Goshirakawa attempted to play one military or Samurai class clan against another, hoping to maintain the prestige and power of the imperial court. Goshirakawa died of illness in the spring of 1192 after which Minamoto no Yoritomo (1147-1180) became the Samurai

47   During this period, Japan had a secondary "monarchy" that was more powerful than the imperial court.

class ruler of Japan. During his lifetime Yoritomo was unable to obtain the imperial commission as *Sei-i tai shogun,* a title widely known as *Shogun,* a position which carried practically dictatorial powers and which he ardently desired both for its prestige and practical advantage. The political game he played was to support the plot of Minamoto no Yoshitsune (1159 – 1189), Yoritomo's half-brother in order to assemble force against Yoritomo's force. Yoshitsune's coup against Yoritomo failed, but Goshirakawa slyly escaped any blame from Yoritomo's force. Yoshitsune was driven out from Kyoto and eventually killed as a traitor by Yoritomo's army. Goshirakawa survived because he didn't use any clear language to support the rebellion. He exercised extremely advanced skills to imply supporting the rebellion without using clear language, so that he could escape from a backlash when the rebellion failed.

Thus, extremely higher-context court culture and covert and subtle language that require keys to interpret were in fact an inheritance Emperor Hirohito (1901 – 1989)[48], who reigned over Japan during the Second World War, received from his ancestors. During his entire life Hirohito kept on using this enigmatic, culturally encrypted language which only his family members or closest associates possessed the tools to decrypt. For instance, when he made a decision to appoint Hideki Tojo as the prime minister of Japan. [49]Hirohito quoted an ancient Chinese Proverb "If you don't go into the cave of the tiger, how are you going to get its cub?" People in Japan's pre-war establishment interpreted this as he tried to use Tojo as a "tiger cub" to stop the war. However, there was no certainty that that was what Hirohito truly intended to say. Koichi Kido, the Lord Keeper of the Seal, must have known the emperor's true intended meaning.

---

48   Wikepedia: Hirohito (裕仁). Online at http://en.wikipedia.org/wiki/Hirohito
49   Ikuhiko Hata. Gendaishi no soten [Controversies of Today's History] pp. 238-253

But he may have sealed any information disagreeing with Hirohito's pacifist public image after the war.

[50]In addition, on November 8, 1941, Hirohito received detailed information about the Pearl Harbor attack plan and commented that their plan was extremely bold and impressive like that of the Battle of Okehazama in which Oda Nobunaga, a medieval warlord, eventually became the ruler of Japan. Bix, author of *Hirohito and the Making of Modern Japan*, understands his statement literally that it was the expression of praise and agreement with the military strategy. But Hirohito's loyalists in Japan might defend him by saying that Hirohito's statement was a sarcastic or indirect expression of disapproval of the plan. It is extremely difficult for almost anyone to understand the true intention of the emperor.

After the war, Hirohito emphasized that he had no authority to influence what took place in the imperial conference. The great majority of Japanese population believed that Hirohito was a real pacifist who was totally against the war with no interest in the expansion of the empire. They blindly believed his statement to [51]Hidenari Terasaki (1900–1950), former First Secretary of the Japanese Embassy in USA, that Hirohito was a "prisoner and powerless puppet of the militarists". Terasaki compiled Hirohito's statements shortly before he died and posthumously coauthored Hirohito Monologue with his daughter Mariko Terasaki Miller (1932 -). But many critics have challenged the view that he was merely a puppet or helpless figurehead. [52]Peter Wetzer contends that the reliability of his postwar statement must be re-examined. Weltzer views that although establishing individual responsibility for specific

---

50   Herbert P. Bix Hirohito and the Making of Modern Japan
51   Hidenari Terasaki & Mariko Terasaki Miller, eds., Showa Tenno Dokuhakuroku [Monologue of Showa Emperor]. (Tokyo: Bunshun Bunko, 1995)
52   Peter Wetzler. Hirohito and War (Honolulu: University of Hawaii Press, 1998) p. 38

decisions was not a clear-cut matter in prewar Japan, Hirohito participated in the decision to start the war.

Wetzer also quotes [53]Akira Fujiwara who did a careful study on the emperor's involvement in critical decision-makings. Fujiwara viewed that the premise that the emperor could not reverse cabinet decisions was a myth fabricated after the war. He found considerable evidence that the emperor briefed Army and Navy's leaders regularly and sanctioned Japan's critically important military decisions during the Second World War, including the plan to attack Pearl Harbor.

Super-Polite Expression

Japan's敬語 (keigo) or super-polite expressions that are uniquely Japanese expressions stem from the Confucian tradition and values and include honorific verbs and extra-modest verbs which represent the higher-context nature of Japanese language. [54]The "super-polite" is a term invented by Tatsuya Nagashima in the late 1970s. The term indicates extremely courteous and honorable expressions that are uniquely Japanese. The Japanese language has standard expressions with verbs which end in "desu" and "masu", informal style expressions with short-form endings of verbs, adjectives and nouns, and the politest expressions that Japanese use when they address their customers and superiors.

The largest part of super-polite expressions is the usage of special verbs which describe the action of respectful people and the modesty of the speaker. First group of verbs are called honorific verbs and express honor to respected people. These verbs are applied to the second and third persons only, since Japanese has the tradition to be modest about himself or herself while giving honors to respect others. Following are examples of honorific verbs:

---

53   Akira Fujiwara, Showa Tenno no Jugo-nen Senso [The fifteen-year war of Showa Emperor]. (Tokyo: Aoki Shoten, 1991)

54   Tatsuya Nagashima, Japanese in 30 Weeks I: Romanji Course. (Tokyo, Japan: PanaLinga Institute, 1980)

Standard Verbs	Honorific Verbs (Dictionary Form)	Masu-Form
いる iru (to be/stay) 行く iku (to go) 来る kuru (to come)	いらっしゃる (irassharu)	*いらっしゃいます (irassha-i-masu)
見る miru (to see)	ご覧になる (goran-ni-naru)	ご覧になります (goran-ni-nar-i-masu)
言う iu (to say)	おっしゃる (ossharu)	*おっしゃいます (ossha-i-masu)
する suru (to do)	なさる (nasaru)	*なさいます (nasa-i-masu)
食べる taberu (to eat) 飲む nomu (to drink)	召し上がる (meshi-agaru)	召し上がります (meshi-agar-i-masu)
くれる kureru (to give to the speaker)	下さる (kudasaru)	*下さいます (kudasa-i-masu)
寝る neru (to sleep)	お休みになる (oyasumi-ni-naru)	お休みになります (oyasumi-ni-nar-i-masu)
~ている teiru (continuing action/ change of a state)	~ていらっしゃる (te-irassharu)	*~ていらっしゃいます (te-irassha-i-masu)

All of these honorific verbs are u-verbs with "ru" endings in the dictionary form, but some of them with an asterisk have an irregularity to drop the "r" at the end of the stem in masu-form. All others conjugate in the same way as regular u-verbs. The honorific verbいらっしゃる (irassharu) is very broad and encompasses actions to be, to go and to come to a respected person.

Some of these honorific verbs might carry an underlying philosophical assumption to regard certain respected individuals to be higher than others. For instance, the respectful counterpart of the verb 食べる (taberu) or to eat is 召し上がる (meshi-agaru) which implies that the person who consumes food is in a position higher than others. The verb "meshi-agaru" is also applied to the consumption of liquid instead of solid objects. The literal meaning is "the food or drink is going up" as it is consumed by an honorable person. Seemingly, the verb has a semantic linkage with "ageru" or to give which stems from "akeru" or "sun is rising". The underlying philosophical assumption of both "ageru" and "meshi-agaru" in Confucianism is to honor others and think that they are higher than the speaker, since these expressions indicate that the object is going up to the higher position when it goes to an honorable person. Particularly, the latter is an expression through which one might pay special tribute and honor to respected individuals like teachers, superiors at work, the elderly and customers.

The honorific version of "kureru" introduced in Chapter Six is 下さる (kudasaru), as the Kanji indicates. The expression also carries an idea that the object goes down when the speaker is the recipient and intensifies the respect to the person who gives. On the other hand the honorific counterpart of "ageru" is 差し上げる (sashi-ageru) and is a compound verb of差し (sashi) which indicates a configuration of hands to hold an object and上げる (ageru) or lifting it up. Just as "kudasaru", it also intensifies the respect and honor to the respected person in the social hierarchy. There is no honorific version of "morau" because the speaker identifies himself or herself with the recipient of an object in "morau", and it is not acceptable to apply the honorific to an action when the speaker is the agent. However, "morau" has an extra-modest expression 頂く (itadaku) to be introduced later.

The honorific version of Te-form and "iru/imasu", which indicates continuing action and change of a state, is Te-form and "irassharu/irassha-i-masu".

There are honorific expressions with the completely identical format as the passive voice that take the verb stem + "a-reru" for u-verbs, and "rareru" ending for ru-verbs. Just like the passive voice, this format is antithetical to "ranuki kotoba" of the potential forms, since "ra" is added to both u-verbs and ru-verbs. The examples of the "a-reru" and "rareru" ending honorific verbs are on the following page.

Just like the passive voice, in "a-reru" and "rareru" ending honorific expressions, u-verbs have "areru" endings that are very similar to re-verbs instead of the "eru" ending. Regarding ru-verbs and the irregular verb "kuru", the passive voice is identical with the potential forms. For another irregular verb "suru", there is no drastic irregularity as in the potential form, but the vowel of the stem is simply shifted from "u" to "a". The sentence structure is Subject + Agent of Action + に (ni) + Direct Object + を (o) + Passive Voice Verb. The subject is often omitted just as in many Japanese sentences, and the direct object is present only with transitive verbs.

A-reru & rareru Ending Honorific Verbs (Short-Forms)

	Dictionary Form	Present Short Affirmative	Present Short Negative	Past Short Affirmative	Past Short Negative
U-Verbs	帰る kaer-u (Return home)	帰られる kaer-a-reru	帰られない kaer-a-renai	帰られた kaer-a-reeta	帰られなかった kaer-a-renakatta
Ru-verbs	食べる mi-ru (eat)	食べられる tabe-rareru	食べられない tabe-rarenai	食べられた tabe-rareta	食べられなかった tabe-rarenakatta
Irregular Verbs	来る ku-ru (come)	来られる ko-rareru	来られない ko-rarenai	来られた ko-rareta	来られなかった ko-rarenakatta
	する su-ru (do)	される sare-ru	されない sare-nai	された sare-ta	されなかった sare-nakatta

4

ADVANCED LEARNERS, JAPAN FOUNDATION STANDARD & CAN-DO (SIX LEVELS OF COMPETENCY)

Introduction to Japan Foundation Standard

The Japan Foundation Standard (JF Standard) for Communicative Language Competencies is designed to evaluate Japanese language learners' competency to communicate, a standard to grade the ability to use Japanese language as a tool of communication.

In fact, almost all beginners and intermediate level learners have not reached A1 or the lowest level of Can-do. Therefore, this scaling system is mainly for students who have completed two volumes of Genki textbooks[55] or the equivalency after spending a minimum of two years in a Japanese language classroom at a college or university. Can-do will promote, encourage and challenge those who have acquired enough vocabulary and knowledge in the writing system and grammar to plunge into the Japanese speaking environment in which they are required to use the language as a part of the daily living instead of simply a subject to study. They must initiate both pragmatic and experimental learning in the realm beyond their horizon instead of a college classroom setting. Can-do will assist these ambitious advanced learners to set clear objectives and goals to develop their

55   Eri Banno, Ono, Yutaka, et al. Genki: An Integrated Course in elementary Japanese I, Vol. 1 & 2, (Tokyo, Japan: Japan Times Press, 1999/2002)

language competencies in a Japanese speaking environment in which a completely new phase of learning takes place.

JF Standard Objectives

JF Standard aims at *Japanese language for mutual understanding,* and holds to the objectives to measure the following competencies of learners. These are *task performance competency* and *cultural understanding competency.* The task performance competency is an overall linguistic competency which encompasses areas like literacy, vocabulary, syntax or grammar. It is a simple measurement to judge ability to speak a language per se as well as a cultural understanding competency includes a wide range of knowledge and understanding of history, politics, religions and entertainment of the host culture along with the language itself. JF Standard maintains the position that Japanese language learners in advanced levels must develop these two areas simultaneously, since language and culture are inseparable.

Communicative Language Competency & Communicative Language Activities

In the JF Standard guide book[56], Communicative Language Competencies include *linguistic competencies, socio linguistic competencies* and *pragmatic competencies* (p. 3-4). JF Standard maintains that all three competencies are equally important and essential for the holistic development of communicative language for advanced level learners.

Linguistic competencies include competencies in vocabulary, grammar, enunciation, literacy such as character recognition and construction. These are basic and foundational factors for any language study and belong to the beginner and intermediate level courses which students must acquire during the first two years in

---

56   JF Standard for Japanese-Language Education 2010 User's Guide. (Saitama, Japan: Japan Foundation, 2010)

college or university classrooms. They were considered the most essential and pivotal factors in language education from the previous era.

Socio-linguistic competencies are an ability to use a language in appropriate social settings. One must use the language appropriately depending on a relationship he or she has with others. In the beginner and intermediate level classrooms, teachers may blend the socio-linguistic approach with the traditional linguistic teaching method with a greater emphasis on grammar and writing competencies. The more advanced the students' language competency, the greater benefit they obtain from the emphasis on socio-linguistic competency development. For advanced students, the focus of Can-do, socio-linguistic competencies are the most central and pressing learning factors, since they must continue to acquire language skills through daily interactions with classmates, colleagues at work, spouses and family members who speak the Japanese language.

Pragmatic competencies include *discourse competencies* and *functional competencies*. Discourse competencies are abilities to construct and control a discourse or a story. Functional competencies are abilities to properly understand the purpose and aim of the use of a language. Examples of functional competencies are the abilities to report and explain facts.

Communicative Language Competency & Long-term Survival for Foreign Students

In 2012, [57]Tomi Harada (2012) conducted an intriguing research on the relationship between language competencies and social skills among foreign students with European and American origin. The sample studied consisted of 69 foreign students with either European or North American origin in Kobe, Japan. The duration of research was

57   Tomi Harada. European and American foreign students' Japanese competence and social skills for cultural social adaptation. (Unpublished Research Presentation in CAJLE Conference in Banff, Canada, 2012)

eight months, and the researcher conducted the survey in the fifth and eighth month after the arrival of the students.

The language competencies in Harada's study were linguistic competencies by JF Standard definition, which include competencies in vocabulary, grammar, enunciation and literacy, such as character recognition and construction. On the other hand, JF Standard maintains that social skills and cultural adaptation belong to the realm of socio-linguistic competencies. Harada's study indicates that when students arrive in Japan, there is a very positive relationship between their linguistic competencies and the level of cultural adaptation to the society. However, as they stay longer, their understanding of the relationship between these factors increases in complexity. Students are required to have more than just "language skills" for survival if they stay longer.

In her research, Harada came to the conclusion that the longer students stay, the more socio-linguistic factors play an important role in students' adaptations to the host culture alongside linguistic competencies in a traditional sense. Harada calls this socio-linguistically vital factor for cultural adaptations "social skills". She also divides social skills into two categories. One is universally applicable and the other is culturally specific. Culturally specific social skills include proper usage of keigo (敬語) or super-polite expressions to their superiors and non-verbal expressions like bowing, smiling in an appropriate context, and the manner to pour beer or sake for superiors and customers.

The study also revealed a negative correlation between the level of student language competencies and the satisfaction with their homestay environment. The results indicated that students with higher competencies in the language were inclined to have lower levels of satisfaction with the living environment in the host culture. It might imply that students with higher language competencies possess more independent spirits, pride in their own achievements and higher expectations of themselves and others, so that they are not easily satisfied. The study also indicated a positive correlation between lower language competencies and dependency on peers as well as satisfaction with their homestay environment.

The overall implication of Harada's study is that the basic language competencies or linguistic competencies in JF Standard definition are the basis to build effective communication skills for foreign students or new immigrants. However, when students stay in Japan longer and get involved in the community more deeply, they require socio-linguistic, or, "social skills" along with language skills.

Social skills are universally applicable factors that are most basic and cannot be neglected anywhere on the planet. For instance, it is socially inappropriate for a man to meet a woman and ask her to marry him in the same day that he first met her. It is a universally applicable rule that human relationships need a certain length of time to grow. It is also universally unacceptable to talk about sex, urination and excretion during meals and anytime in front of strangers. Some of these factors might have stemmed from prehistoric memories, the most ancient part of humanity or physiology of the spices *Homo sapiens sapiens*. Human brains are likely programed by the creator to feel unpleasant when they are forced to be in certain situations. No matter whether one is a foreigner or native to a land, he or she will not be considered socially appropriate while being ignorant of these factors. If a man asks a woman to marry him at the moment of meeting her, there is virtually no chance that she says "yes" unless she has a different physiology than humans.

On the other hand, foreign students and new immigrants must follow many culturally specific rules in the process of developing any kind of relationship. These rules stem from more recent memories inherited from our ancestors. Foreign students and any other kind of newcomers to the land must be familiarized with culturally specific part of the "social skills" like *keigo* (敬語) or super-polite expressions to their superiors and non-verbal expressions like bowing. These rules are newer than universal rules and developed during the written history of mankind. As mentioned earlier, the custom to use polite expressions to superiors and the elderly in Japan and other East Asian regions most likely stems from Confucian ideology. Confucianism, with its great emphasis on the importance of social hierarchies and respect for elders and leadership, is a nearly 2500 year old philosophy and prevalent over two millennia. When Japanese leadership introduced writing systems and technologies in the seventh century, they also imported Confucian political philosophy and utilized it to govern the nation. There is a debate if the original teaching of Confucius (551–479 BC) had the same emphasis on these social hierarchies such as obedience to authorities and respect for leadership in the same way as medieval and modern teachers in Japan and China. It seems that the teaching of Great Confucius has been modified and conveniently used by government authorities in East Asia including Japan.

There is no doubt that the modified version of Confucianism that was prevalent in the whole of East Asia throughout two millenia contributed to the formation of the culturally specific "social skills" in Japan. It is this culture of *keigo*, rigid social hierarchies in corporations and other socio-linguistic elements that cause enigma for European and North American students.

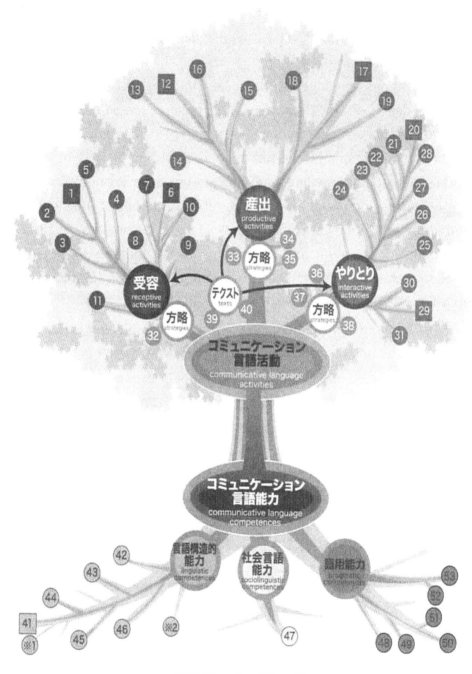

[58]JF Standard Tree[59].

58   JF Standard for Japanese-Language Education 2010. (Saitama, Japan: Japan Foundation, 2010) pp.8

59   The picture is used under "fair dealing" (Canada) and "fair use" (USA) provisions in copyright law.

JF Standard Tree

JF Standard manual[60] as well as its guide book[61], includes a tree shaped diagram named JF Standard Tree, in which the relationship between various language competencies and language activities is plainly described (p. 9, manual). As we observe the shape of the tree, the place for communicative language competencies is the bottom of the stem. Underneath, there is a room divided into three segments that are linguistic competencies, socio linguistic competencies and pragmatic competencies. At the top of the stem and above the section of communicative language competency, there is a section of communicative language activities that are divided into three branches. These branches are receptive activities, productive activities and interactive activities.

The communicative language competencies are described as the root of a tree and consist of the following three components. The first part is linguistic competencies include competencies in vocabulary, grammar, enunciation, literacy such as character recognition and construction. The second part is socio-linguistic competencies that are concerned with abilities to use a language in appropriate social settings. The third part is pragmatic competencies, or ability to construct discourses and understand their roles and objectives.

The communicative language activity stands upon the communicative language competencies and expands like branches of a tree. Each of these branches consists of receptive activities, productive activities and interactive activities.

Can-do Levels of JF Standard

JF Standard includes a measurement scale of the Japanese language competencies named *Can-do*. Can-do is a detail

---

60   JF Standard for Japanese-Language Education 2010. (Saitama, Japan: Japan
     Foundation, 2010)
61   JF Standard for Japanese-Language Education 2010 User's Guide. Ibid.

measurement that JF Standard adopted to evaluate student competency and is divided into six scales. Students can take advantage of Can-do for self-diagnosis of their language competency and their progress of learning. In my opinion, Can-do is also a very effective tool for these advanced students to set goals and objectives of continuous learning.

Can-do includes three main levels of language competencies, in which each of them is broken into two sub-levels (p. 8). The lowest and most rudimentary level among them is A1 (p. 9).

The A1 level students are the lowest among advanced learners and usually those who have completed the intermediate level of Japanese outside of Japan. They possess a considerable amount of knowlege of grammar, vocabulary and writing systems, however lack experiences to practice their knowlege in real-time situations. They are able to produce and comprehend very short sentences with a limited number of vocabulary in both written and spoken language. They have enough competencies to satisfy the basic and minimum needs of daily living such as grocery shopping, finding public restrooms and introducing themselves to others. With a strict control of vocabulary to be used, A1 learners are able to engage in a brief dialogue. Generally speaking, those without East Asian heritage who have completed Introductory and Intermediate level (first two years) of Japanese language courses in a North American college or university might possess the A1 level competency (p. 8-9). If they are enrolled as International students from Korea or China, their learning process could be faster to achieve the A1 level significantly faster than indigenous students. Likewise, North American born students with Chinese or Korean parentage may progress faster than indigenous Caucasian students[62].

---

62   JF Standard for Japanese-Language Education 2010 User's Guide. Ibid.

A2 is a slightly more advanced level than A1 and those in this level are able to manage slightly longer and more complicated sentences than the A1 level. A2 level learners are able to read, write, listen and be engaged in a simple conversation more smoothly than A1 learners. A2 learners are also able to make brief presentations of well-studied materials with well written manuscripts and rehearsals. After a presentation, they are able to answer questions if they are simple enough and consist of limited and controlled vocabulary (p. 8-11). North American college or university students with Chinese or Korean heritage often achieve A2 level or higher when they have completed the first two years of Japanese.

B1 level is a significantly more advanced level than the first two levels. The B1 level learners are able to comprehend a wider range of topics centered around school, work and entertainment, if the speakers use standard Japanese. B1 learners also possess a higher level of competency in presentations or public speaking than A2 level learners. B1 learners are able to present the subject matter in which they are well versed, clearly and logically in front of an audience. On agreeing or disagreeing with someone else's views, they are able to state reasons for their choice. If they have several alternatives, they are able to state pros and cons of each.

C1 level learners are able to comprehend and present very complex and highly academic subject matters fluently. They are able to defend their viewpoints highly persuasively and win arguments in highly academic subjects. They are also able to answer adequately any unexpected questions of the audience.

C2 level learners could be classified as extremely advanced achievers in learning Japanese. They have even higher competencies than the average native speakers in many different ways. They have the ability to present highly academic subject matters in plain Japanese in front of non-academic audiences. They are able to present many different subject matters competently in front of almost all types of Japanese speaking audiences.

Utilizing Can-do in Language Learning Settings

Can-do may be utilized in various Japanese language learning settings for mostly advanced learners either in or outside of classrooms. First, Can-do is an effective tool to set concrete and specific learning objectives and goals for each person (p. 15). The goals and objectives may be custom made, varying based on the personal needs and circumstances. Each learner or teacher may visit the [63]Can-do web site and find the most relevent item for him or her to develop certain types of language skills and use it to design a lesson.

For instance, a learner may set an objective to develop the ability to use *keigo* (敬語) or super-polite expressions in a business environment. Those in Japanese speaking business environments require much more knowledge in polite expressions than expressions taught in a textbook. In fact, a person who is employed in Japanese corporations, particularly in service industries, is required to know the wider range of polite expressions. This learning is in addition to the basics of super-polite expressions usually taught in the intermediate level (second year) class in North American colleges and universities. They need to combine these polite expressions with other non-verbal expressions important in business. He or she may set a learning goal in which the polite expressions must be nearly perfect, while his or her overall language performance may stay at A1 or A2.

A person in the hard sciences or the medical field, however, must set the goal to B1 or higher when discussing scientific topics, while he or she may have A1 or A2 level competency in other topics. If a person is in a medical or nursing profession and intends to practice in Japan, he or she must be able to comprehend and explain fluently topics in a specialized field, therefore requires minimum B2 level language

---

63   Can-do web site (みんなの「Can-do」サイト). Online at http://jfstandard.jp/

competency dealing with natural science. Fluency on other topics is desirable, but not a priority for this person.

Can-do may also be utilized to evaluate the learning process of each learner. It is a good tool for teachers to use to grade students' progress as well as students' self-evaluation. Both parties may get together to discuss the learning progress using Can-do as a measurement. It is also helpful to re-examine the learning goals per se and determine if it is beneficial for a learner to continue learning[64].

As Can-do is utilized as a tool to set goals and evaluate the learning process of students, the selection of good learning materials is most vital and pivotal. Since there is no standard textbook for advanced learners, a teacher must be careful to select proper and relevant material for each learner. Each teacher may be innovative to select learning materials, contextualizing and integrating them with Can-do Standard.

Example: Utilizing Can-do to Design Courses

Can-do is flexible to allow the freedom to modify, re-write or re-format Can-do to fit any learning objectives. The first task is to make use of the Can-do in learner's own unique circumstances in creating a list of learning objectives. The process may follow the next five steps (p. 49-53).

These steps are 1) brainstorming and searching for the most relevant Can-do category for his or her student 2) visiting [65]JF Standard's own web page "みんなの 「Can-do」 サイト" and selecting a Can-do category from the list of items 3) selecting several of the most relevant sub-categories from the Can-do category that he or she has chosen 4) rewriting Can-do into easier Japanese or translating it into the student's native language 5) reformatting Can-do sub-categories as a new document with identical learning topics and objectives, but slightly different orientation that students utilize for

64   JF Standard for Japanese-Language Education 2010 User's Guide. Ibid.
65   Can-do web site. Ibid.

their learning including the course or lesson title and length of time for the learning to take place.

A translated Can-do document for a new course design may be utilized effectively when more than two students with the same mother tongue study together. When the whole matrix for a new course is formatted as an official document or translated into a different language, the teacher/author may copyright it as a new intellectual property. The copyright could either belong to the teacher exclusively, or when student(s) and teachers are regarded as joint author(s).

For instance, a teacher may select B1 category in which a student is able to comprehend and express most topics in his or her academic fields as well as almost all other topics of daily living. The teacher and student may set two goals under this category. The first would be to deepen knowledge and understanding of the Japanese way of thinking and customs and how average Japanese people comprehend and perceive the student's native land and its culture. By doing this, the student may reach a deeper understanding and awareness of similarities and differences between the Japanese and student's native cultures. The second goal would be to develop the ability to converse with Japanese people, mainly acquaintances at work, on a wide variety of topics using plain expressions and occasionally discussing similarities and differences between Japanese and the culture of student's native land (p. 53)[66].

On the Can-do site, the teacher surveys the most relevant topic under the B1 category. Then, the teacher would assign the topic "jibun to kazoku" (自分と家族) or "self and family" to his or her student. Then, the teacher and student would set the objective that the student should be able to discuss his or her strengths and weaknesses to a certain extent in front of newly acquainted Japanese people.

---

66   JF Standard for Japanese-Language Education 2010 User's Guide. Ibid.

Example:

Utilizing Can-do to Create Measurement for Speech Ability

Next, the Japanese language teacher and his or her students may utilize Can-do as a powerful instrument in the process of creating a standard of evaluation and measurement of spoken Japanese, since it has several different levels of accomplishment in the course of learning the language (p. 57). The process to create a standard may take the following steps.

First, the teacher must determine what kind of components of the student's ability will be evaluated. The components of speech competency to be observed may be the way that the topic developed, logical consistency and coherency of the speech, range and proper usage of vocabulary, correct grammar and intonation. Next, the teacher and his or her student must decide the level of Can-do which is applied for the evaluating process. They may decide to use the range of A2 to B1, and divide it into four grades. The lowest grade is entitled "ganbatte" (がんばって) or "work harder". The second grade is "moo sukoshi" (もうすこし) or "do a little more". The third one is "dekita" (できた) or "done". The fourth and highest grade is "subarashii" (すばらしい) or wonderful. The first two levels are in the A2 level and the second two levels are B1 level (p. 60).

In creating a measurement to evaluate a student's performance, the teacher must create a new document with a new format. As the teacher has divided both A2 and B1 into two sub-levels. For instance, if he or she is going to divide A2 into A2.1 and A2.2 sub-levels, the contents of each of them may be the following:

A2.1 level learners possess basic skills to use Japanese conjunctures like "soshite" (そして) or "and", "shikashi" (しかし) or "but", "dakara" (だから) or "because" to integrate several expressions into one sentence. On the other hand, A2.2 level learners are able to utilize Japanese conjunctures to construct more sophisticated sentences with more elaborate and detailed descriptions. They are also able to utilize most frequently used conjunctures to create their own discourses with better continuity and coherency than what A2.1 learners created (p. 61)[67].

In completing the whole process, the document may also be rewritten into easier Japanese or translated into a student's native language the same way as creating the Can-do based course design matrix. Along with a document of evaluating measurement, a teacher may create a one page evaluation sheet for teachers and students. When the entire document and evaluation sheet are made, the teacher/writer may also copyright them as a new intellectual properties at the end. He or she may be either the sole author or share the authorship with his or her student(s).

Can-do & Cross-Cultural Experts

Above all, the JF Standard and Can-do will assist those who have immigrated to a Japanese speaking environment after completing college level intermediate Japanese courses in their respective homelands. Their new learning environment is completely different from typical classroom settings. These individuals who dive into a Japanese speaking environment will maximize the new learning instruments in a whole course of pragmatic, experimental and socio-linguistic learning experience. Their main objective would be the preparation of further academic or vocational careers and to start a new life in a totally different cultural milieu or environment instead of simply learning a language.

Those who have resided in Japan for significantly long periods and developed their careers successfully may reach C2 or the highest point of Can-do with equivalent or higher competency than the

---

67   JF Standard for Japanese-Language Education 2010 User's Guide. Ibid.

average Japanese native speakers. These individuals are also well versed in the history, politics, religions, entertainment and pop culture in Japan.

[68]Typical accessories in Japanese homes.

---

68   The picture is taken by the author, 2009.

Part 2

GRAMMAR, WRITING, AND EDUCATION DEVELOPMENT

NOTES

5

INTRODUCTORY JAPANESE GRAMMAR VS. ENGLISH GRAMMAR

Omitting Subject

The grammar and word order of Japanese and English are different in many ways. For those who grew up in the English speaking world and are accustomed to the English word order and way of thinking, Japanese syntax must be very perplexing and difficult to comprehend. In modern English, the subject is a very essential part of a sentence and it is nearly impossible to create a sentence without a subject. In a Japanese sentence, however, the subject, direct object or any other nouns are omitted whenever the speaker thinks them unnecessary. If it is clear what is being discussed, nouns including subjects or direct objects are abbreviated. In the first dialogue of the Genki textbook that I have used in class since 2002, the character named Takeshi asks Mary, the main character of the book, りゅうがくせいですか (Ryuugakusee desu ka) or "Are you an International student?" Then, Mary responds, ええ、アリゾナだいがくのがくせいです。 (Ee, Arizona daigaku no gakusee desu) or "Yes, (I) am a student at the University of Arizona". Takeshi did not make a full statement, あなたはりゅうがくせいですか (Anata wa ryuugakusee desu ka). As Takeshi asks Mary a question, he did not state the subject "anata' which means "you" and the particle "wa" which would come at the beginning of his statement in English, because it is obvious whom he is talking about. Likewise, as Mary responded to Takeshi, she did not state the subject "watashi' and the particle "wa" which would come in English at the beginning of her statement, because it is also very clear whom she is talking about[69].

"I Thee Wed" Syntax

In my own wedding ceremony in May 2014, the pastor asked me to address my bride with a classic English sentence "I thee wed" prior to placing a ring on her finger. I wrote it down on my palm, since I was so nervous that I might forget the statement during the ceremony. I found the syntax of this short statement intriguing because unlike modern English, the verb "wed" was placed at the end. I also found that this sentence and the Japanese syntax had a common feature. Japanese always has the verb or copula at the end of the sentence, while modern English has the predicate next to the subject. I call this sentence pattern the "I Thee Wed" syntax found in middle and some early modern English, but never seen in contemporary English[70].

An example of a simple sentence which ends with a noun + copula is "太郎は犬です" (Taro wa inu desu), which means "Taro is a dog". An example of a simple sentence which ends with a verb is "ロバートさんは大阪でそばを食べます" (Robaato san wa Osaka de soba o tabemasu), which means "Robert eats soba (noodle) in Osaka". Unlike English, both copulas and verbs which form the predicate come at the end of the sentence in Japanese. In modern days, it makes Japanese syntax very unique and distinct from both Chinese and Indo European family languages including English. (Soba - p. 182)

---

69   Eri Banno, Ono, Yutaka, et al. Genki: An Integrated Course in elementary Japanese I, Vol. 1, (Tokyo, Japan: Japan Times Press, 1999/2002)

70   The direct Japanese translation of "I thee wed" is 私はあなたと結婚します (Watashi wa anata to kekkon shimasu). The verb "kekkon shimasu" comes at the end of the sentence.

Case Indicating Particles

Japanese language has "case indicating particles" and "sentence final particles" which make the language unique. In Japanese, cases of the noun are determined by placing one of several particles after it, while in English they are determined by the word order and the uses of prepositions like "to", "in", "at" and "of". After the subject, either は "wa" or が "ga" must be placed depending on the situation as I briefly introduced in the Chapter One. Then the particle を "o" must be placed after the direct object. Particle に "ni" is very versatile and is normally placed after a time reference or a destination. The particle "ni" also comes after an indirect object or after the noun considered dative in Latin and Greek grammar. Examples of uses of "ni" for the time references are:

a) メアリーさんは八時<u>に</u>おきます。 (mearii san wa hachiji <u>ni</u> okimasu). "Mary wakes up at 8 o'clock" b) たけしさんは日曜日<u>に</u>うどんを食べます。 (takeshi san wa nhichiyobi <u>ni</u> udon o tabemasu). "Takeshi eats udon on Sunday" c) 山下さんは９月<u>に</u>南瓜を食べます。 (yamashita san wa kugatsu <u>ni</u> kabocha o tabemasu). "Yamashita eats pumpkins in September".

The first sentence is an example of the use of "ni" with numerical time like hours and minutes. The second sentence is an example of the use of "ni" with a day in a week. The third sentence is an example of the use of "ni" with a month. Several time related expressions in relation to the present moment like 'kyoo" (今日) "today", "ashita" (明日) "tomorrow" or "kinoo" (昨日) "yesterday" do not accompany the particle "ni". Today is today only for today. In tomorrow, tomorrow is today and today is yesterday and yesterday is the day before yesterday. Also, time related adverbs which points out the frequency of some events like "mainichi" (毎日), "maiban" (毎晩), "maishu" (毎週) or "maitoshi" (毎年) do not accompany "ni". The equivalency of the particle "ni" coming after the time reference in English is "at" (hours

and minutes), "on" (days and weeks) and "in" (months and years).
These prepositions come before the noun, while Japanese particles
come after the noun[71]. The particle "ni" is also used to indicate the
direction of the movement and examples follow:

a) けんさんは明日学校に行きます。(Ken san wa ashita gakko
ni ikimasu). "Ken goes to school tomorrow". b) メアリーさんは１２
月にアメリカに帰ります。(Mearii san wa jyuuni gatsu ni amerika
ni kaerimasu). "Mary returns to America in December". In the first
sentence, "ni" after "gakko" or school, indicates that the school is his
destination of the verb "ikimasu" which means to go. In the second
sentence the particle "ni" comes twice. The first appearance is for
the time reference or December, and the second appearance is for
the destination that she returns. The equivalency of the particle "ni",
coming after the noun for the destination in English is "to", "into" and
"toward". Besides the particle "ni", another particle "e" (へ) is used
to show the direction or destination. This particle has only one way of
being used. The hiragana "へ" is usually pronounced "he", but only
when it is used as a particle, it is pronounced "e". These two particles
are almost always interchangeable, but with slightly different nuances.
An example to compare sentences with different nuances of "ni" and
"e" are as follows:

b) たけしさんは東京スカイツリーに行きます。(Takeshi san
wa Tokyo Sukai Tsurii ni ikimasu) "Takeshi is going to Tokyo Skytree" b)
たけしさんは東京スカイツリーへ行きます。(Takeshi san wa Tokyo
Sukai Tsurii e ikimasu) "Takeshi is going toward Tokyo Skytree". The
first sentence simply reports a fact that Takeshi is heading to Tokyo
Skytree", a well-known landmark in the Japanese capital. The second
sentence has the same meaning as the first, but with more emphasis
on the direction or "towardness" that he is heading to in the same way
as the English translation indicated.

71　Since the case indicating particles are placed after the noun, some grammarians
　　call them "post-positions".

The particle "de" (で) generates the equivalency of the locative and instrumental cases in Latin and Greek grammar. The locative case follows indication of the location that certain events and activities will take place or after the noun considered locative in Latin and Greek grammar. The English equivalency of "de" is also "at", "on" and "in." The examples of uses of "de" coming after the location in which certain events take place are as following:

a) たけしさんは家で晩御飯を食べます。 (Takeshi san wa ie de bangohan o tabemasu). "Takeshi eats supper at home" b) 真理子さんは喫茶店で勉強します。 (Mariko san wa kissaten de benkyo shimasu). "Mariko studies at a coffee shop" c) 田中さんは明日東京でお酒を飲みます。 (Tanaka san wa ashita Tokyo de osake o nomimasu). "Tomorrow, Tanaka drinks sake in Tokyo".

In the first sentence, the particle "de" indicates the location that Takeshi eats his supper, and that it is at his home because "de" is before "ie" or home. In the second sentence, the particle "de" tells that the location Mariko studies is a coffee shop, since the particle is located after the noun "kissaten" which means "coffee shop". In the third sentence, the particle "de" indicates the location in which Tanaka drinks sake tomorrow is Tokyo, since it comes after the location word Tokyo. It is simply because "at" comes prior to smaller places, while at the same time "in" comes prior to larger places in English. However, the particle "de" consistently comes after the location of activities no matter how big it is.

The particle "de" also appears after the instrumentative case, or a noun for an object that someone uses as an instrument case. The following sentence is an example in which "de" is used in the instrument case. はしで御飯をたべます。 (Hashi de gohan o tabemasu). "(I) eat meal with chopsticks. The particle "de" indicates that "hashi" or chopsticks are instruments for eating meals.

The particle "to" (と) generates the equivalency of the concomitative case in Latin and Greek grammar. It appears when two nouns or pronouns are combined or compared to each other. Examples of sentences with the particle "to" are the following: a) 私は明日ロバートさんと晩御飯を食べます。(Watashi wa ashita Robaato san to bangohan o tabemasu). "Tomorrow, I am going to eat supper with Robert" b) トロントで肉と野菜を買います。(Toronto de niku to yasai o kaimasu). "I am buying meat and vegetables in Toronto. 東京の食べ物と京都の食べ物は違います。(Tokyo no tabemono to Kyoto no tabemono wa chigaimasu). "Tokyo's food and Kyoto's food are different". In the first example, "to" is translated into "together with" and describes the "togetherness" of people or animate beings. In the second sentence, the particle combines two items and carries an idea that the speaker buys meat and vegetables together. In the third sentence, the particle compares and contrasts two items such as Tokyo's food and Kyoto's food.

The Japanese language also has three more particles "kara" (から), "yori" (より) and "made" (まで). The particle "kara" (から) generates the equivalency of ablative case in Latin and Greek grammar. It can be translated into "from" or "off" in English depending on the context. Examples of sentences with the particle "kara" are the following: a) 東京から名古屋にいきます。(Tokyo kara Nagoya ni ikimasu). "(I) go to Nagoya from Tokyo" b) 歌舞伎は１２時から４時までです。(Kabuki wa jyuuniji kara yoji made desu). "Kabuki takes from 12 o'clock to 4 o'clock" which means the particle "kara" indicates a spatial–temporal starting point, and comes after the noun for the location and time. In the first sentence the particle "kara" is placed before the location word "Tokyo" and indicates that Tokyo is the starting point of a journey. In the second sentence, "kara" is placed after the numerical time that the Kabuki performance starts.

There is also the second "kara" which indicates the reason. Sentences which include "kara" explain the reason or the cause of a certain situation. Examples of sentences with the second "kara" are the following:

a) 明日テストがありますから、私は今日勉強します。 (Ashita tesuto ga arimasu kara, watashi wa kyoo benkyoo shimasu). "Because there is a test tomorrow, I will study today". b) 新幹線は高いからバスに乗ります。 (Shinkansen wa takai kara basu ni norimasu). "Because the bullet train is expensive, (I) go by bus". In the first sentence, "kara" indicates the reason that the speaker of the sentence studies. In the second sentence, the statement before "kara" tells the reason that he or she is using a bus instead of the bullet train.

The particle "yori" (より) is another comparative case indicator with the similar function as the English "more than". It compares and contrasts two items and tells which one is superior or inferior, longer or shorter, larger or smaller, etc. The particle is also used with the phrase "no hooga" (のほうが). The examples of uses of "yori" to compare two items are the following: a) 中国語のほうが韓国語より難しいです。 (Chuugoku go no hoo ga Kankoku go yori muzukashii desu). "Chinese language is more difficult than Korean language" b) 東京のラーメンのほうが名古屋のラーメンよりおいしいです。 (Tokyo no ramen no hooga Nagoya no ramen yori oishii desu). "Tokyo's ramen (noodle) is more delicious than Nagoya's ramen (noodle). As the sample sentences indicate, the syntax of a sentence is noun 1 + "no hooga" + noun 2 "yori" + adjective + desu. (Ramen - p. 189)

The particle "made" (まで) is translated into "up to" or "until" in English and considered the equivalent of limitative case in Latin and Greek grammar, and indicates the spatial–temporal limitation, destination or finishing point. The examples of uses of "made" to tell the boundary and finishing point in time and place are as follows: a)

私は駅まで歩きます。(Watashi wa eki made arukimasu). "I will walk to the (train) station". b) 6 時まで日本語を勉強します。(Rokuji made nihongo o benkyoo shimasu). "I will study the Japanese language until 6 o'clock". The first sentence is an example that "made" used with a verb of movement indicates the geographic destination. The particle "ni" in the second sentence indicates the ending time of duration. When the "made" is used for a destination in a geographic sense, it is often interchangeable with "ni" or "e", but with different nuances, since "made" has a strong emphasis on the "finishing point".

The following sentences compare the nuances of "ni", "e" and "made": a) けんさんは秋葉原に電車で行きます。(Ken san wa Akihabara <u>ni</u> densha de ikimasu) "Ken is going <u>to</u> Akihabara by train" b) けんさんは秋葉原へ電車で行きます。(Ken san wa Akihabara <u>e</u> densha de ikimasu) "Takeshi is going <u>toward</u> Akihabara by train" c) けんさんは秋葉原まで電車で行きます。(Ken san wa Akihabara <u>made</u> densha de ikimasu) "Takeshi is going <u>up to</u> Akihabara by train". The first sentence which accompanies "ni" sinply states that Ken's destination is Akihabara, the holy ground of Otaku people, and he is going there by train. The second sentence with "e" has a nuance that the direction to Akihabara is more emphasized just like the previous example I have introduced. The third sentence with "made" has an emphasis that Akihabara is Ken's final destination. He will not simply pass by the town, but stay there for certain duration of time.

Present & Past Tenses of Adjectives & Nouns

Adjectives, nouns and verbs have tenses (present and past), polarities (affirmative and negative) in Japanese. However, unlike English, Japanese verbs and copulas (adjectives' and nouns' endings) do not form with corresponding verb endings that distinguish the speaker (first person), the individual addressed (second person), and the individual or thing spoken of (third person). Japanese has no concept of the "persons" with three roles which distinguishes the speaker, the addressee, and the individual or thing being referenced. The language also does not form corresponding verb inflections based on numbers, and most Japanese nouns have no distinction between singular and plural. The language has two distinct adjectives ("i" and "na" adjectives) with different conjugational patterns. Nouns conjugate exactly in the same pattern as na-adjectives. The present tense in Japanese often describes future events and is translated into the future tense, when a sentence is translated into English.

To introduce desu-form (standard expression for adjectives and nouns) present tense of adjectives and nouns, the tables underneath indicate conjugation patterns of i-adjectives and na-adjectives. An example of i-adjective is おもしろい (omoshiroi), which means "interesting":

I-Adjective Present Tense

おもしろい omoshiroi	Affirmative	Negative
Present	おもしろいです omoshiroi desu	おもしろくないです omoshirokunai desu
English Translation	(It) is interesting/They are interesting	(It) is not interesting/They are not interesting

The stem of おもしろい (omoshiroi) is おもしろ (omoshiro) and all i-adjectives have "i" ending, dictionary form. The present tense affirmative is formed by addingいです(idesu) to the stem, and negative by adding くないです(kunai desu). An example of na-adjective is げんきな (genkina) which means "healthy" or energetic".

Na-Adjective Present Tense

元気な genkina	Affirmative	Negative
Present	元気ですgenki desu	元気じゃないです genki janai desu
English Translation	(He/she) is healthy/ They are healthy	(He/she) is not healthy. They are not healthy

The table underneath introduces the masu-form present tense conjugation of a noun 学生 (gakusee) which means "student".

Nouns Present Tense

学生gakusee	Affirmative	Negative
Present	学生です gakusee desu	学生じゃないです gakusee janai desu
English Translation	(He/she) is a student/ They are students	(He/she) is not a student/They are not students

The na-adjectives conjugate in the same way as nouns because they were originally nouns and are still able to be used as nouns. For instance "genki", introduced in the second table, is an example of na-adjectives also functioning as a noun. As a noun, "genki" carries a meaning of "health" or "energy". The expression 元気がないです (genki ga naidesu) means "there is no energy". Nagashima (1980) called na-adjectives "noun adjectives" in his textbook, because they were originally nouns[72].

To introduce the past tense of these adjectives and nouns, it's important to go back to the i-adjective "omoshiroi" which means "interesting". The following table is the past tense conjugation of "omoshiroi".

I-Adjective Past Tense

おもしろい omoshiroi	Affirmative	Negative
Past Tense	おもしろかったです omoshirokatta desu	おもしろくなかったです omoshirokunakatta desu
English Translation	(It) was interesting/ They were interesting	(It) was not interesting/ They were not interesting

---

72   Tatsuya Nagashima, Japanese in 30 Weeks I: Romanji Course. Ibid.

In the masu-form, past tense of i-adjectives, the "i desu" at the end is replaced by "katta desu".

Na-Adjective Past Tense

元気な genkina	Affirmative	Negative
Past Tense	元気でした genki deshita	元気じゃなかったです genki janakatta desu
English Translation	(He/she) was healthy/ They were healthy	(He/she) was not healthy/ They were not healthy

Nouns Past Tense

学生gakusee	Affirmative	Negative
Past Tense	学生でしたgakusee deshita	学生じゃなかったです gakusee janakatta desu
English Translation	(He/she) was a student/ They were students	(He/she) was not a student/ They were not students

For na-adjectives and nouns, "desu" is replaced by "deshita" in the present tense and "ja naidesu" is replaced by "nakattadesu.

I-Adjective's Conjugational Endings

	Affirmative	Negative
Present Tense	いです idesu	くないです kunaidesu
Past Tense	かったです katta desu	くなかったです kunakatta desu

Na-Adjective's & Nouns (Copula) Conjugational Endings

	Affirmative	Negative
Present Tense	です desu	じゃないです janaidesu
Past Tense	でした deshita	じゃなかったです janakatta desu

Just like English and all other languages, Japanese has present and past tenses, affirmative and negative polarities. However, the simpler and easier part of the language is that the verbs do not form with corresponding verb endings that distinguish the speaker, the individual addressed, and the individual or thing referenced.

Kunaidesu vs. Kuarimasen

In the negative, there is also an alternative and slightly more dated variant くありません (ku arimasen) for the present and くありませんでした (ku arimasen deshita) for the past tense instead of くないです (ku naidesu) and くなかったです (ku nakatta desu) for i=adjectives. For na-adjectives and nouns, じゃありません (ja arimasen) for the present and じゃありませんでした (ja arimasen deshita) for the past tense instead of じゃないです (ja naidesu) and じゃなかったです(ja nakatta desu). Almost all Japanese textbooks published before 2010 that included the first edition of Genki introduced the older "ku arimasen/ ja arimasen" endings to students as the most important expressions. However, when Genki released the second edition, some of the contents were drastically revised and "ku arimasen/ja arimasen" endings of adjectives and nouns were replaced by "ku naidesu/ja naidesu".

Masu-Form Present & Past Tenses of Verbs

The masu-form (standard expression for verbs) refers to the present tense of verbs. In the Japanese language there are three kinds of verbs. The first group is called "u-verbs" because the inflectional ending is only one vowel "u", and there is one vowel infix or the middle part before the inflection. The second class of Japanese verbs is called "ru-verbs". For ru-verbs, inflectional ending is "ru" or one syllable insted of one vowel "u". In addition, Japanese has two irregular verbs 来る (kuru) "to come" and する (suru) "to do." The following table presents the masu form of present tense of ru-verbs.

The word みる (mi-ru) means to see as an example of ru-verb, because the conjugation of ru-verbs is simpler than u-verbs. Just as adjectives and nouns in English, Japanese verbs do not form different inflections[73] based on the roles of persons and distinction between singular and plural.

Ru-Verb Present Tense

みる mi-ru	Affirmative	Negative
Present	みます mi-masu	みません mi-masen
English Translation	I, you or they see/he or she sees	I, you or they do not see/he or she does not see

For ru-verbs, the conjugation pattern is simple so that one can create the present tense affirmative of masu-form by replacing the suffix "ru" with "masu" and the negative polarity by replacing it with "masen". This is similar to to converting the affirmative into the negative in which the last "su" is replaced with "sen".

Examples of sentences which include the present tense affirmative and negative of "mi-ru" are as follows:

a) メアリーさんは京都で映画を見ます。(Mearii san wa Kyoto de eega o mimasu). "Mary watches a movie in Kyoto" b) 次郎さんは家でテレビを見ません。(Jiro san wa ie de terebi o mimasen). "Jiro does not watch TV at home".

---

73 I use terminologies like inflection, inflectional ending and suffix interchangeably. All of them indicate the final inflectional part of verbs and adjectives which take different forms on conjugations.

Both sentences follow the same format, with the subject + wa, location word + de, direct object + o, and the ru-verb "mimasu" or "mimasen". The verb "miru" always takes one or more direct objects followed by the particle "o", since it is a transitive verb. If you want to state more than two direct objects, you must use the particle "to" between them and make a sentence like this. ナンシーさんは大阪で映画と歌舞伎を見ます。(Nanshii san wa Osaka de eega to Kabuki o mimasu). "Nancy watches a movie and Kabuki (theatre) in Osaka"[74].

On the other hand, the conjugation of u-verbs is a little more complex since the stem often ends in a consonant and the inflection is only the vowel "u" in the dictionary, as per the following table:

U-Verb Present Tense

飲む nom-u	Affirmative	Negative
Present	飲みます nom-i-masu	飲みません nom-i-masen
English Translation	I, You or they drink/He or she drinks	I, You or they do not drink/He or she does not drink

The suffix or the inflectional ending of u-verbs is just a vowel in the dictionary form. When the present tense affirmative of masu-form is created, you must take off the last vowel "u" and keep the consonant "m". After removing "u", you need to add an infix or middle part "i", and then add "masu". When you are making the negative, you must follow the same rule to add the infix "i" but "masen" comes at the end instead of "masu". In this part, you can follow the same rule as ru-verbs to add "masem" instead of "masu". Likewise, in converting the affirmative into the negative, you simply replace the last "su" with "sen". Japanese also has a couple of irregular verbs. Examples of sentences which include the present tense affirmative and negative of the u-verb "nom-u" follow:

74 歌舞伎 (Kabuki) is a traditional Japanese theatrical art.

a) メアリーさんは東京の居酒屋で焼酎を飲みます。(Mearii san wa Tokyo no izakaya de shoochuu o nomimasu). "Mary drinks shochu (Japanese vodka) in a Izakaya Pub in Tokyo"
b) トムさんはビールをぜんぜん飲みません。(Tomu san wa biiru o zenzen nomimasen). "Tom doesn't drink beer at all".

The first sentence includes the present tense affirmative of nomu which means to drink. "Nomu" like "miru" is a transitive verb, so that it must take at least one direct object. This time, the direct object is "shochu", a popular alcoholic beverage in Japan because of its minimum carbohydrate content and excellent taste. Izakaya is the location word coming with a locative particle "ni" which indicates where she drinks "shochu". The second sentence includes the present tense negative of the same verb. The adverb "zenzen" literally means "not at all" and comes with negative expressions only. (Izakaya-p. 182)

The next couple of tables are for the present tense masu-form conjugation of the two:

Irregular Verb Present Tense (Kuru)

くる (kuru)	Affirmative	Negative
Present	きます ki-masu	きません ki-masen
English Translation	I, You or they come/He or she comes	I, You or they do not come/He or she does not come.

Irregular Verb Present Tense (Suru)

する (suru)	Affirmative	Negative
Present	します shi-masu	しません shi-masen
English Translation	I, you or they do/He or she does	I, You or they do not come/He or she does not do

These are considered irregular verbs since their stems change, but otherwise the conjugational patterns are similar to ru-verbs. For "kuru" the stem "ku" is shifted into "ki", but the consonant "k" stays the same and the real change is only the vowel after the consonant. For "suru" the stem "su" is shifted into "shi", but the consonant "s" stays the same and the real change is only the vowel after the consonant. The reason to add an extra "h" between "s" and "i" is that the Japanese language does not have a "si" sound. These irregular verbs also act almost in an identical way as ru-verbs when they form the negative except a shift of the stem vowel. In order to form the negative, you simply have to add "masem" instead of "masu", just as any other Japanese verbs. Likewise, in converting the affirmative into the negative, you simply replace the last "su" with "sen".

The examples of sentences which include the present tense of "kuru" and "suru" are as follows:

a) メアリーさんは水曜日に名古屋に来ます。 (Mearii san wa suiyoobi ni nagoya ni kimasu). "Mary cames to Nagano on Wednesday" b) みちこさんは土曜日に学校に来ません。 (Michiko san wa doyoobi ni gakkoo ni kimasen) "Michiko didn't come to school on Saturday" c) けんさんは日曜日に家で洗濯します。 (Ken san wa nichiyoobi ni ie de sentaku shimashu). "Ken does laundry at home on Sunday" d) 田中さんはスポーツをしません。 (Tanaka san wa supootsu o shimasen). "Tanaka doesn't play sports".

The first and the second sentences include the affirmative and negative present tense of "kuru", and the stem "ku" turns into "ki". Days of the week like"suiyoobi" (Wednesday), "doyoobi" (Saturday) and "nichiyoobi" are followed by the particle "ni". The third and fourth sentences include the affirmative and negative present tense of "suru". In the same way as the present tense, the stem "su" turns into "shi". Also, we may call "suru" a "verbalizer" to create a new verb by joining a noun. "Sentaku-suru" is a compound verb in which "suru" means to "do" joined to the noun "sentaku" or "laundry". In the last sentence, the noun "supootsu" or "sports" is considered a direct object of "shimasen" or the negative of "suru" instead of forming a combined verb, because there is an accusative case indicator particle "o" after "supootsu". However, it is also possible to make a statement "supootsu-shimasen" in which the two of them are merged instead of saying "supootsu o shimasen".

Now, let's look at the past tenses of Japanese verbs in the following tables.

Ru-Verb Past Tense

みる mi-ru	Affirmative	Negative
Present	みました mi-mashita	みませんでした mi-masen-deshita
English Translation	I, you, he, she or they saw	I, I, you, he, she or they did not see

In the past tense, the ru-verbs conjugation pattern is simple like the present tense, so that you can create the past tense affirmative of masu-form by replacing the suffix "ru" with "mashita" and the past tense by replacing it with "masen-deshita". As discussed, "mashita" shares the same first syllable "ma" and the following consonant "s" with "masu", the present tense ending. When you want to convert the present to the past tense, all you have to remember is to replace the last vowel "u" with "ita". For the negative, you simply have to add "deshita" after the present tense ending "masen". Examples of sentences which include the past tense affirmative and negative of "mi-ru" follow:

a) クリスティーさんは横浜から東京タワーとスカイツリーを見ました。(Kuristii san wa Yokohama kara Tokyo tawaa to Sukai Tsurii o mimasita). "Kristy saw Tokyo Tower and Skytree from Yokohama" b) 次郎さんは図書館でビデオを見ませんでした。(Jiro san wa toshokan de bideo o mimasen- deshita). "Jiro did not watch TV at home".

The first sentence includes the past tense affirmative of the ru-verb "miru". It also includes the location word + kara (from) and two direct objects linked together by the particle "to". In this sentence, the location word Yokohama accompanies the particle "kara" which means "from" instead of an ordinary "ni". It carries an idea that Kristy viewed something in the distance from Yokohama. The second sentence includes the past tense negative of the same verb and a location word "toshokan" (library) + the particle "ni" which indicates the location where Jiro did not watch TV.

When creating the past tense of u-verbs, you need to follow the same pattern. Please look at the following table:

U-Verb Past Tense

のむ nom-u	Affirmative	Negative
Past	のみました nom-i-mashita	のみませんでした nom-i-masen-deshita
English Translation	I, you, he, she or they drank	I, you, he, she or they did not drink

After removing the suffix "u" from the dictionary form and adding the infix "i", you can follow the exact same pattern as the re-verb past tense. You need to create the past tense affirmative of masu-form by replacing the suffix "ru" with "mashita" and the past tense negative by replacing it with "masen-deshita". You can also apply the same rule to convert the present to the past tense by replacing the last vowel "u" with "ita". Examples of sentences which include the past tense affirmative and negative of the u-verb "nom-u" are as follows:
a) 山下さんは東京の下北沢でビールをたくさん飲みました。
(Yamashita san wa Tokyo no Shimokitazawa de biiru o takusan nomimashita). "Yamashita drank a lot of beer in a Shimokitazawa in Tokyo"

b) たけしさんは月曜日にお茶を余り飲みませんでした。(Takeshi san wa getsuyoobi ni ocha o amari nomimasen-deshita). "Takeshi didn't drink tea that much on Saturday".

The first sentence includes the past tense affirmative of nomu which means to drink. This time, the direct object is "biiru" or beer, and "takusan" is an adverb which indicates a big quantity used for both countable and uncountable items. (Shimokitazawa - p.182)

The second sentence includes the past tense negative of the same verb. The adverb "amari" literally means "not much" and comes with negative expressions like "zenzen" which means "not at all." "Getsuyoobi" or "Monday" is followed by the particle "ni" because it is a day of a week. Following are examples of the past tense of irregular verbs:

Irregular Verb Past Tense (Kuru)

くる (kuru)	Affirmative	Negative
Past	きました ki-<u>mashita</u>	きませんでした ki-<u>masendeshita</u>
English Translation	I, you, he, she or they came	I, you, he, she or they did not come

Irregular Verb Past Tense (Suru)

する (suru)	Affirmative	Negative
Past	しました shi-<u>mashita</u>	しませんでした shi-<u>masendeshita</u>
English Translation	I, you, he, she or they did	I, you, he, she or they did not do

Just as in the present tense, you can follow the exact same pattern as the ru-verb past tense. For "suru" the stem す "su" is shifted into し "shi", but the consonant "s" stays the same and the real change is only the vowel after the consonant. For "kuru" the stem "ku" is shifted into "ki", but the consonant "k" stays same and the real change is only the vowel after the consonant[75]. The examples of sentences which include the past tense of "kuru" and "suru" follow:

a) ロバートさんはきのう名古屋に来ました。(Robaato san wa kinoo nagoya ni kimashita). "Robert came to Nagoya yesterday" b) メアリーさんは先週学校に来ませんでした。(Mearii san wa senshuu gakkoo ni kimasendeshita) "Mary didn't come to school last week" c) たけしさんは金曜日に部屋をそうじしました。(Takeshi san wa kinyoobi ni heya o sooji shimashita). "Takeshi cleaned his room on Friday" d) 山下さんは学生のころ余り勉強しませんでした。(Yamashita san wa gakusee no koro amari benkyoo shimasen deshita). "Yamashita didn't study that much when he was a student".

The first and the second sentences include the affirmative and negative past tense of "kuru". Just as the present tense, the stem "ku" turns into "ki", the time reference word "kinoo" which means yesterday, does not take the particle "ni" since it is a word in relation to "now" or the present moment. In the same way "senshuu" or the "last week" does not take "ni". The third and fourth sentences include the affirmative and negative past tense of "suru". In the same way as the present tense, the stem "su" turns into "shi". As mentioned before, "suru" is a "verbalizer" to create a new verb by joining to a noun. "Sooji-suru" is a compound verb "suru" which means "to do" joined with the noun "sooji" or a cleaning activity of properties. "Benkyo-suru" is a compound verb that "suru" joined the noun "benkyo" or "study". Therefore, "sooji-suru" literally means "doing house cleaning" and "benkyoo-suru" literally means "doing study". The former is the verbalization of the noun "sooji" or an activity to clean homes and the latter verbalizes "benkyo" or "study". The adverb "amari" literally means "not much" and comes with negative expressions like "zenzen".

---

75   They follow the same rules as in the present tense.

Just as the present tense, there is also an alternative to insert the particle "o" between a noun and the verb "suru", and treat nouns like "sooji" or "benkyo" as direct objects of "suru".

Summarizing the masu-form conjugation of all Japanese verbs, the table at the end of this section will display the suffix or conjugational endings of present and past tense, affirmative and negative of all Japanese verbs. Ru-verbs, u-verbs and irregular verbs have different ways of forming the stem and infix or the middle part. Ru-verbs drop the last syllable from the dictionary form and do not change except for the suffix or the endings. U-verbs drops only the last vowel "u" from the dictionary form and add the middle part "i", before adding the end. Irregular verbs are similar to ru-verbs, except the vowel of the stem shifts into "i" from "U'. However, all of these verbs have the same universal endings when they are in masu-forms.

Japanese Verb's Conjugational Endings

	Affirmative	Negative
Present Tense	ます masu	ません masen
Past Tense	ました mashita	ませんでした masendeshita

In the same way as adjectives and nouns, an easy part of Japanese verbs is the absence of the difference among first, second and third persons and distinction between singular and plural. The Japanese verbs do not form with corresponding verb endings that distinguish the speaker, the individual addressed, and the individual or thing spoken of.

Short-Form vs. Desu/Masu Forms

As stated in the previous chapter, Japanese has informal and super-polite endings of verbs and adjectives besides standard "masu" endings for verbs and "desu" endings for adjectives and copula. Informal expressions are commonly used among family members or close friends at school or work. In informal settings, they employ the style of speech called short-forms. In short-forms nouns and verbs have a different paradigm of conjugation from masu-forms. When you get to know people well enough, you may start using short forms as you converse with them. However, it is not easy to know an appropriate time to switch to short forms. Also, regarding a permission of using short forms when one is addressing others at school and work, age and seniority matters. Senior partners at work may feel it is acceptable to address in the short form to younger partners, while expecting the juniors to continue to address in "masu" and "desu" ending expressions, since license to use short form is not necessarily mutual[76]. This custom to use different styles of expressions depending on relationships with people, is most likely due to nearly 2500 years of Confucianism philosophy with its strong emphasis on the importance of social hierarchies and respect to elders and loyalty to masters.

Short-Form Present & Past Tenses of Adjectives & Nouns

Let's look at an example of short-form conjugation of i-adjectives isおいしい (oishii) which means "delicious":

I-Adjective Present Tense (Short-Forms)

おいしい oishii	Affirmative	Negative
Present	おいしい oishi-i	おいしくない oishi-kunai
English Translation	(It) is delicious	(It) is not delicious

As shown, the present tense affirmative of i-adjectives is identical to the dictionary form. For the negative, it is the same as the standard form except the final "desu" is dropped. The following sentences are examples of short-form present tense affirmative and negative including the i-adjective "oishii".

---

76   Eri Banno, Ono, Yutaka, et al. Genki: An Integrated Course in elementary Japanese I, Vol. 1. Ibid.

a) 築地のレストランはおいしい。(Tsukiji no resutoran wa oishii). "Tsukiji's restaurants are delicious".

b) 長野のさかなはおいしくない。(Nagano no sakana wa oishikunai). "Nagano's fish are not delicious".

Following are past tense short-forms of i-adjectives:

I-Adjective Past Tense (Short-Forms)

おいしい omoshiroi	Affirmative	Negative
Past	おいしかった omoshi-katta	おいしくなかった oishi-kunakatta
English Translation	(It) was delicious	(It) was not delicious

Fot the past tense, the final "i" of the affirmative and the "kunakatta" of the negatives are replaced with "katta" and "kunakatta" respectively. The following sentences are examples of short-form present tense affirmative and negative including the i-adjective "oishii".

a) 銀座のとんかつはおいしかった。(Ginza no resutoran wa oishi-katta). "Ginza's Tonkatsu was delicious"

b) 田舎のラーメンはおいしくなかった。(Inaka no ramen wa oishikuna-katta). "Ramen (noodle) in the countryside was not delicious".

The following two tables display examples of na-adjectives' and nouns' short-form present tenses. They show the present tense affirmative and negative of a na-adjective and nouns with "kireina" and "neko".

Na-Adjective Present Tense (Short-Forms)

きれいな kireina	Affirmative	Negative
Present	きれいだ kirei-da	きれいじゃない kirei-janai
English Translation	It/she is beautiful/They are beautiful	It/she is not beautiful/ They are not beautiful

Nouns Present Tense (Short-Forms)

猫neko	Affirmative	Negative
Present	猫だneko-da	猫じゃない neko-janai
English Translation	I am a cat/ You/they are (a) cat (He/she) is a cat	(He/she) is not a cat You/they are not (a) cat

In short-forms, the present tense affirmatives of na-adjectives and nouns normally end in "da" unlike "i" adjectives. For the negative, they end in "janai" in the same way as i-adjectives. The endings are the same as the standard desu-form except the final "desu" is dropped. Examples of sentences which include present tense affirmative and negative of na-adjectives and nouns are the following:

a) 沖縄の海はきれいだ。(Okinawa no umi wa kireida). "Okinawa's sea is beautiful"

b) 東京の川はきれいじゃない。(Tokyo no kawa wa kirei janai). "Tokyo's rivers are not beautiful"

c) にゃんたはたけしの猫だ。(Nyanta wa Takeshi no neko da) Nyanta is Takeshi's cat".

The first sentence includes the subject "Okinawa no umi" or "sea of Okinawa" and the present tense affirmative of the na-adjective "kireina". The second sentence includes the subject "Tokyo no kawa" or "rivers in Tokyo" and the present tense negative of the na-adjective "kireina". "Tokyo no kawa" literally means "rivers in Tokyo", but a better translation is "rivers in Tokyo" because the particle "no" is more versatile than prepositions like "of", "in" or "at" in English. In fact, these rivers are located in Tokyo and Tokyo does not own them.

Although short-form affirmatives of nouns and na-adjectives normally end in "da", there is one occasion that "da" is omitted. When used in constructing interrogatives and answers, the final "da" for the affirmative is dropped. Examples are the following:

a) 隅田川の花火きれい？ (Sumida gawa no hanabi kirei). "Are fireworks by Sumida River beautiful?" うん、きれい。(un, kirei). "Yes, it is beautiful" b) これはあなたの猫？ (Kore wa anata no neko) "Is this your cat?" うん、ぼくの猫。(Un, bokuno neko). "Yes, this is my cat".

The questions and affirmative answers omit the final "da" as you see the examples above. However, the negative answers take the same form as the simple statement similar to the following:

a) ううん、きれいじゃない。 (Uun, kirei janai). "No, it's not beautiful" b) ううん、ぼくの猫じゃない。 (Uun, boku no neko janai). "No, he is not my cat".

The next two tables show the past tense short-forms of "kireina" and "neko".

Na-Adjective Past Tense (Short-Forms)

きれいな kireina	Affirmative	Negative
Past	きれいだった kirei-datta	きれいじゃなかった kirei janakatta
English Translation	It/she is beautiful/They are beautiful	It/she is not beautiful/They are not beautiful

Nouns Past Tense (Short-Forms)

猫neko	Affirmative	Negative
Past	猫だったneko-<u>datta</u>	猫じゃなかった neko-<u>janakatta</u>
English Translation	I He/she was a cat/ You, they were a cat	I, He, she was not a cat. You, they were not a cat

In short-forms, the past tense affirmatives of na-adjectives and nouns end in "datta" unlike "i" adjectives which end in "kata". For the negative, they end with "janakatta" while i-adjectives end in "kunakatta". Examples of sentences which include past tense affirmative and negative of na-adjectives and nouns are the following:

a) 神田川は昔きれいだった。(Kanda gawa wa mukashi kireidatta). "Kanda River was beautiful a long time ago" b) 墨田川はきれいじゃなかった。(Sumida gawa wa kirei janakatta). "Sumida River was not beautiful".

The first sentence includes the subject "kanda gawa" or Kanda River and the present tense affirmative of the na-adjective "kireina". The sentence expresses the way the river was in the past. The adverb "mukashi" means "a long time ago" and it does not take the particle "ni" because "a long time ago" is a relative expression in relation to the present moment and not referencing the remote past. (Kandagawa River - p. 183)

Short-Form Present & Past Tenses of Verbs

Just like i-adjectives, the present tense affirmative of all verbs is identical to the dictionary form for the short-form present tense of verbs. Likewise, for the negative, it is also the same as the standard form except the final "desu" drops. Let's start from the ru-verb conjugation. Following is the conjugation table of the short-form present tense of ru-verbs:

Ru-Verb Present Tense (Short-Forms)

食べる tabe-<u>ru</u>	Affirmative	Negative
Present	食べる tabe-<u>ru</u>	食べない tabe-<u>nai</u>
English Translation	I, You or they eat/He or she eats	I, You or they do not eat/He or she does not eat

For ru-verbs, the conjugation pattern is even simpler than masu-forms. The affirmative is identical with the dictionary form, and you can create the negative by replacing the last "ru" with "nai". You may also remember that if you want to convert the affirmative into the negative, you simply replace the last "ru" with "nai".

Examples of sentences which include the short-form present tense affirmative and negative of "tabe-ru" are as follows:

a) ナンシーさんは京都ですっぽんを食べる。(Nanshii san wa Kyoto de suppon o taberu). "Nancy eats suppon (soft-shell turtle) in Kyoto" b) たけしさんはこわいから家でふぐを食べない。(Takeshi san wa kowai kara ie de fugu o tabenai). "Takeshi does not eat blowfish at home because it is scary". (Suppon - p. 183/Blowfish - p. 185)

Both sentences follow the same format, with the subject + wa, location word + de, direct object + o, and the short-form present tense of the ru-verb "taberu". Both sentences also take a direct object, because the verb "miru" always takes one or more direct objects followed by the particle "o", since it is a transitive verb. The verb of the first sentence is the same as the dictionary form, since present tense short-forms of any verbs and i-adjectives are identical with the dictionary forms. Next, let's look at the present tense short-form of u-verbs with a minor difference from the short forms of ru-verbs.

U-Verb Present Tense (Short-Forms)

のる noru	Affirmative	Negative
Present	のる noru	のらない nor-a-nai
English Translation	I, You He or she or they ride	I, You, he or she or they do not ride

For the u-verb short-form present tense, the affirmative is identical with the dictionary form just like the ru-verb. However, for the negative, the vowel "u" is dropped and the infix "a" added before the suffix "nai". For instance, 新幹線は高いから乗らない。(Shinkansen wa takai kara nor-a-nai). "(I) do not ride Shinkansen or bullet train because it is expensive" includes the short-form present tense of the u-verb "noru" with slightly different conjugation from ru-verbs. (Shinkansen - p. 193)

The next two tables represent the short-form present tense of irregular verbs.

Irregular Verb Short-Forms Present Tense (Kuru)

くる (kuru)	Affirmative	Negative
Present	くる ku-ru	こない ko-nai
English Translation	I, you, or they come/ he or she comes	I, you, or they do not come/ he or she does not come

Irregular Verb Short-Form Present Tense (Suru)

する (suru)	Affirmative	Negative
Present	する su-ru	しない shi-nai
English Translation	I, you, or they do/ he or she does	I, you, or they do not do/ he or she does not do

In order to make irregular verb's short-form present tense, you can follow the exact same pattern as the re-verb except the stem change of the negative. Unlike masu-form, the stem change does not happen in the affirmative, since it is identical to the dictionary form. For the negative, the vowel after "s" shifts to "i" from "u" and adds "s" between them since Japanese does not have the "si" sound. Examples of sentences which include the short-form present tense of "kuru" and "suru" are as follows:

a) 田中さんは木曜日に名古屋に来る。(Tanaka san wa mokuyoobi ni nagoya ni kuru). "Tanaka comes to Nagano on Thursday" b) たけしさんは土曜日に私の家に来ない。(Takeshi san wa doyobi ni watashi no ie ni konai) "Takeshi does not come to my home on Saturday" c) けんさんとロバートさんは土曜日に公園でバレーボールをする。(Ken san to Robaato san wa doyoobi ni kooen de bareebooru o suru). "Ken and Robert play volleyball in a park on Saturday" d) トムさんはぜんぜんそうじをしない。(Tomu san wa zenzen sooji o shinai). "Tom doesn't clean (his place) at all".

The first and the second sentences include the short-form affirmative and negative present tense of "kuru", and the stem "ku" turns into "ko" in the negative, while the affirmative is completely identical with the dictionary form. Also, the third and the fourth sentences include the short-form affirmative and negative present tense of "suru", and the stem "su" turns into "shi" in the negative, while the affirmative is identical to the dictionary form. Japanese uses "suru" which means "to do" for any sports including volleyball. They do not say "play volleyball", but rather "do volleyball". In the last sentence, the adverb "zenzen" is linked with a negative predicate only and indicates Tom does not clean his place at all and lives a "pig's lifestyle".

The following represents the past tense short-forms of the ru-verb "taberu":

Ru-Verb Past Tense (Short-Forms)

食べる tabe-<u>ru</u>	Affirmative	Negative
Past	食べた tabe-<u>ta</u>	食べなかった tabe-<u>nakatta</u>
English Translation	I, you, he, she or they ate	I, you, he or she or they did not eat

The past tense affirmative of all verbs has the "ta" ending. For ru-verbs, replace the "ru" ending of the dictionary form and short-form present tense with "ta", the past tense ending. For the negative, you need to replace the "nai" ending of the present tense with the negative "nakatta" ending. Examples of sentences which include the past tense affirmative and negative of ru-verbs are as follows:

a) 日本人は昔うさぎをよく食べた。 (Nihon jin wa mukashi usagi o yoku tabeta). "Japanese people often ate rabbit a long time ago" b) 江戸時代の人は肉を余り食べなかった。 (Edo jidai no hito wa niku o amari tabenakatta). "People in the Edo Period did not eat meat that much". (Japanese Diet during Edo Period - p. 185)

Both sentences follow the format which include the subject + direct object + o, and the ru-verb. The first sentence has an adverb "mukashi" which means "long time ago" between the subject and direct object. The adverb "amari' in the second sentence means "not much" and comes with negative expressions only.

Regarding the short-form past tense, u-verbs have different groups and with various conjugational endings in the short-form affirmative past tense. They are almost identical with "te-forms" (introduced in the next chapter), except the last vowel. In the short-form affirmative past tense the final vowel is "a", while te-form has "e" ending. Four different categories of u-verbs are as follows:

The first group are those which end in "u" (う), "tsu" (つ) and "ru" (る). Examples are "au: 会う" (to meet), "matsu: 待つ" (to wait) or, and "toru: とる" (to take). In the short-form affirmative past tense, they all end with ":ったtta" or the ending with double consonants and "te". Te-form ending of "au: 会う" is "atte: 会った", "matsu: 待つ" is "matta: 待った", and "toru: とる" is "totta: とった". The second group are those with a final ending "mu" (む), "bu" (ぶ) and "nu" (ぬ). Examples are "yomu: 読む" (to read), "asobu: 遊ぶ" (to play) and "shinu: 死ぬ" (to die). They have the "nde: んだ" ending in the te-form. In the te-form, "yomu: 読む" is "yonde: 読んだ", "asobu: 遊ぶ" is "asonde: 遊んだ" and "shinu: 死ぬ" is "shinde: 死んだ". The third group consists of those ending with final "ku" (く), and the example of "kaku: 書く" (to write). The short-form past tense affirmative of "kaku: 書く" is "kaita: 書いた". The only exception among "ku" ending verbs is "iku: 行く" (to go), and its te-form is "itte: 行った". The fourth category is the u-verbs ending with final "gu" (ぐ), and the example is "oyogu: 泳ぐ" (to swim) and the short-form past tense affirmative is "oyoida: 泳いだ". The fifth and last category is those which end with final "su" (す), with the example of "hanasu: 話す" (to speak) and the short-form past tense ia "hanashita: 話した".

A pitfall for many beginners is to assume all verbs with ru-endings in the dictionary form are ru-verbs. However, it is a wrong assumption and numerous "ru" ending verbs are u-verbs. Just like all ru-verbs, many of them have "ru" endings in the dictionary form and many learners find it overwhelmingly difficult to differentiate between the two. Genki does a good job to give a plain enough explanation to learners that that if the vowels "a", "u" or "o" are observed right before the final "ru", they are certainly u-verbs. If the vowels "i" or "e" appear prior to the final "ru", they are usually ru-verbs with some exceptions like "neru" (to sleep) and "kaeru" (to go back).

An example of the past tense short-forms of the u-verb "noru"shows when one of the u-verbs with a ru-ending in the dictionary form. It is an u-verb since the vowel "o" is observed right before the final "ru, as the following table indicates:

U-Verb Past Tense (Short-Forms)

のる nor<u>u</u>	Affirmative	Negative
Past	のった no<u>tta</u>	のらなかった noranaka<u>tta</u>
English Translation	I,you, he, she, they rode	I, you he, she, they did not ride

The past tense short-form affirmative is "notta" with "った:tta" ending (double consonant "tt" and the vowel "a"), since it belongs to the first group in which their dictionary form end in "u" (う), "tsu" (つ) and "ru" (る). Examples of sentences which include past tense affirmative and negative of ru-verbs are as follows:

a) ロバートさんは去年の夏新幹線にのった。(Robaato san wa kyonen no natsu shinkansen ni notta). "Robert rode Shinkansen in the previous summer" b) みちこさんはきのう地下鉄にのらなかった。(Michiko san wa kinoo chikatetsu ni noranakatta). "Michiko didn't ride the subway yesterday".

In both sentences, there is the particle "ni" instead of "o" after the means of transportation. In English, the verb "ride" takes a direct object, and any vehicles like cars, trains, ships and airplanes become a direct object. However, "noru" in Japanese references the fact these vehicles are considered a "destination" to ride or board instead of direct objects. The time reference "kyonen no natsu" (last year's summer) sometimes takes particle "ni" and sometimes doesn't, because it is a hybrid of "kyonen" (last year) relative to the present moment, and "natsu" (summer) that is a more specific time.

Following are the last two tables on the short-form past tense of irregular verbs:

Irregular Verb Short-Forms Past Tense (Kuru)

くる (kuru)	Affirmative	Negative
Past	きた　ki-<u>ta</u>	こなかった ko-<u>nakatta</u>
English Translation	I, you, he, she or they came	I, you, he, she or they did not come

Irregular Verb Short-Form Past Tense (Suru)

する (suru)	Affirmative	Negative
Past	した　shi-<u>ta</u>	しなかった shi-<u>nakatta</u>
English Translation	I, you, he, she or they did	I, you, he, she or they did not do

In order to make irregular verb short-form past tense, follow the same pattern as the re-verb except some stem changes. The examples of sentences which include the short-form past tense of "kuru" and "suru" are as follows:

a) メアリーさんは先週の土曜日に名古屋の明治村に来た？ (Mearii san wa senshuu no doyoobi ni nagoya no Meiji Mura ni kita). "Mary, did you come to Nagoya's Meiji Mura last Saturday?" b) ううん、来なかった。(Uun, konakatta). "No, I didn't come" c) けんさんとロバートさんは土曜日に海でサーフィンをした？ (Ken san to Robaato san wa doyoobi ni umi de saafin o shita). "Did Ken and Robert play surfing in the sea on Saturday?" d) ううん、しなかった。(Uun, shinakatta). "No, they didn't do it".
(Meijimura Museum - p. 193)

The first and the second sentences include the short-form affirmative and negative present tense of "kuru", and the stem "ku" turns into "ki" in the affirmative similar to the masu-form, while the negative is turned into "ko". It is also a dialogue which includes a question and answer. In this case, "Mearii san" is a second person instead of a third person. In Japanese dialogue, a person's name is often used as a second person or a substitute of "anata" which means "you". In response to the question, Mary answered negatively saying, "Uun, konakatta". In this context, the other person is talking about Mary who is there as a second person, unless there is a third Mary. The third and the fourth sentences include the short-form affirmative and in both the affirmative and negative past tense of "suru", the stem turns into "shi". In the same way as volleyball, they do not say to "play surfing", but say to "do volleyball" instead. Just like Mary in the first dialogue, Ken and Robert could be either second persons or third persons.

Different Usages of Short-Forms

Besides the formation of informal and casual style of speech, there are several different ways of using short-form verb endings. For instance, when constructing a long and complex sentence, inside a quotation is normally stated in a short-form. Examples of two types of sentences which include quotations ending in short-forms include a first type ending in と思います (to omoimasu) or "I think that", and the second type ending in と言っていました (to itte imashita) or "someone else said that". The first type assumes a person's thought and the second type quotes his or her utterances.

The structure of the "to omoimasu" sentences consist of Subject + Verbs (short form) or Subject + Adjectives (short form) + と (to) + 思います/思う (omoimasu/omou). If the main clause outside of the quotation is the short form, it has "omou" ending, otherwise it ends in "omoimasu". Examples are as follows:

(私は) たけしさんは天ぷらそばが好きだと思います。
("Watashi wa" Takeshi san wa tempura soba ga suki-da to omoimasu).
"(I) think Takeshi likes soba noodle with Tempura".

When "to omoimasu" ends complex sentences, the subject is usually omitted since it is very clear that the speaker is the subject. Unlike the English equivalency "I think", "to omoimasu" comes at the end of the sentence because of the nature of the language that the predicate comes at the very end. The statement within the quotation is "Takeshi san wa tempura soba ga suki-da" indicates Takeshi's favorite food. It is "da" ending because it includes a short-form present tense of a na-adjective "sukina".

Next, the structure of the "to itte imashita" sentences consist of Subject + Verbs (short form) or Subject + Adjectives (short form) + と (to) +言っていました/言っていた (itte-imashita/itte-ita). An example of the "to omoimasu" type follows. The ending "itte imashita" is an idiomatic expression "someone said that". Grammatically, it has Te-form + "imashita" which is an equivalency of the present perfect tense in English and describes an action which happened at an unspecified time before the present moment. If the main clause outside of the quotation is the short form it has "itte-ita" ending, otherwise it ends in "itte-imashita". In English, the tense within the subordinate clause normally agrees with the main clause of the sentence. However, it is quite common that these two tenses do not agree in complex sentences in Japanese. In this case, the verb tense of the verb within the subordinate clause does not agree with the main clause outside of the quotation. An example of the "to itte imashita" follows:

たろうさんは中国語を話さないと言っていました。Taro san wa chuugokugo o hanasanai to itte-imashita). "Someone said Taro did (does) not speak the Chinese language".

In the "itte-imashita" sentence, it is not clear who the subject is, so that the sentence normally starts with either "someone said" or "they said" when translated into English. However, you cannot exclude the possibility that it is Taro's own statement. If both verbs in the main and subordinate clauses are the past tense, it is a similar setting to the past perfect tense in English and describes events in a "past of the past", or the events that took place prior to the past described in the simple past tense. For example, (私は) たけしさんはレストランでビールを飲んだと思いました。 ("Watashi wa" Takeshi san wa resutoran de biiru o nonda to to omoi-mashita). "(I) thought Takeshi had drunk beer in a restaurant". In this sentence, the speaker had a thought in the past. At the point he or she had a thought, according to the person's thinking, Takeshi had a beer sometime in the past.

There are several other usages of short-forms. For instance, short-form present tense (dictionary form) + のが好きです/きらいです (no ga suki-desu/kirai-desu) is a statement to express one's favor and disfavor. "Sukidesu" is the present-tense affirmative of "sukina", a na-adjective which means to "like" or "favour". On the other hand, "Kiraidesu" is the present-tense affirmative of "kiraina", a na-adjective which means to "dislike" or "disfavour". The examples of sentences which include the short-form present tense and "ga suki-desu" and "ga kiirai-desu" are as follows:

a) メアリーさんは写真を撮るのが好きです。 (Mearii san wa shashin o toru no ga suki-desu). "Mary likes to take pictures" b) ロバートさんは車を運転するのがきらいです。 (Robaato san wa kuruma o unten suru no ga kirai-desu). "Robert hates driving".

The particle "no" after the short-form affirmative (dictionary form) is a "nominalizer" with the equivalent function as "ing" ending which forms a gerund in English.

In the suki-desu/ kirai-desu format, the subject is not the person who likes or dislikes a certain thing. Instead, the subject is the item he or she likes or dislikes. The syntax of the sentence is person + wa + subject (verb's dictionary form/short-form present tense affirmative)

+ ga + suki-desu/kirai-desu. So, the literal meaning of "suki-desu" is "likable" and "kirai-desu" is dislikable. Thus, the literal translation of the first sentence is, "For Mary, photo taking is *likable*".

Besides "suki-desu" and "kirai-desu", there are a couple of other na-adjectives that can be used in the same format. They are 上手です (jyoze-desu) "good at something" and 下手です (heta-desu) "poor or clumsy at something". The examples of sentences which include the short-form present tense and "ga jyozu-desu" and "ga heta-desu" are as follows:

a) たけしさんは泳ぐのが上手です。 (Takeshi san wa oyogu no ga jyozu-desu). "Takeshi is good at swimming" b) みちこさんは歌を歌うのが下手です。 (Michiko san wa uta o utau no ga heta-desu). "Michiko is poor at singing a song".

The syntax of the sentence is person + wa + subject + ga + jyozu-desu/heta-desu, and the subject is an activity to swim or sing, not the person. The literal translation of the first sentence is "Regarding Takeshi, swimming is skillful". The second sentence must be, "As for Michiko, singing a song is poor". The kanji for "jyozu" is a combination of 上 (jyoo) "up" and 手 (zu) "hand" indicating the literal meaning that one's hand is up. This is an idiomatic expression that he or she is skillful at something. On the other hand, the kanji for "heta" is a combination of 下 (he) "up" and 手 (ta) "hand" indicating the literal meaning that one's hand is down. This is an idiomatic expression that he or she is skillful or clumsy at something. So, as Kanji indicates, the meaning of "jyozu-desu" is "being skillful" and "heta-desu" is poor at something. An alternative of "jyozu-desu" is "umai-desu", an expression which includes the i-adjective うまい "umai" with a nearly identical meaning to "jyoozuna". However, there is no alternative to "heta-desu".

This sentence pattern person + wa + subject (verb's dictionary form/short-form present tense affirmative) + ga + adjective + desu expresses a wide range of person's favor or disfavor, and capability and incapability. Also, it is possible to replace the verb's dictionary form/short-form present tense affirmative as a subject with a real noun which indicates an activity. The following example will contrast a sentence with a short-form/dictionary form + no as the subject with another one with a noun as the subject.

a) メアリーさんはすしを食べるのが好きです。(Mearii san wa sushi o taberu no ga suki-desu). "Mary likes to eat sushi".

b) メアリーさんはすしが好きです。(Mearii san wa sushi ga suki-desu). "Mary likes sushi".

These two sentences have nearly identical meanings, except in the first sentence Mary likes an activity to eat sushi, while she likes sushi as an object. However, "liking sushi" almost always means "liking to eat sushi".

Also, the sentence pattern person + wa + subject (verb's dictionary form/short-form present tense affirmative) + ga + adjective + desu is applied to only a few adjectives including "suki-desu", "kirai-desu", "jyozu-desu", "heta-desu" "umai-desu". You cannot make a sentence like "たけしさんはさかなを食べるのがおいしいです"。(Takeshi san wa sakana o taberu no ga oishii-desu). "Takeshi is delicious at eating fish?" It is an extremely awkward and ungrammatical sentence.

However, if the subject is a noun instead of the verb's dictionary form/short-form, there are many other possibilities. Then, the sentence pattern is noun + wa + subject (noun) + ga + adjective + desu. The first noun at the beginning of the sentence may be either a person or a non-person. The following sentences are examples that the first noun is either a person or non-person and end in an adjective as the predicate other than, "suki-desu", "kirai-desu", "jyozu-desu", "umai-desu", and "heta-desu":

a) トムさんは頭がいいです。 (Tomu san wa atama ga ii-desu). "Tom is smart".

b) 京都はうどんがおいしいです。 (Kyoto wa udon ga oishii-desu). "Regarding Kyoto, udon is delicious".

The first sentence is an example that references the person who comes at the beginning of the sentence. In this sentence, "atama ga ii-desu", which is translated into "smart", literally means "head is good". The literal translation of the whole sentence is, "Regarding Tom, the head is good". In this sentence pattern, Tom seems to be a subject although "atama", or his head, is the real subject just as the "suki-desu" and "kirai-desu" type sentences.

The second sentence is an example that a noun for a place instead of a person comes at the beginning of the sentence, and does not seem to be the subject. In this context, udon is the subject in both the technical and practical senses. The particle "wa" can be replaced with either "no" or "de" and still construct grammatically correct sentences. If you state 京都のうどんがおいしいです, (Kyoto no udon ga oishii desu), you can translate the whole sentence,"Kyoto's udon is delicious". If you state 京都でうどんがおいしいです, (Kyoto de udon ga oishii desu), you can translate the whole sentence,"In Kyoto udon is delicious". The first sentence indicates that the delicious udon belongs to Kyoto as a property. The second sentence has more emphasis on the location of Kyoto as a place where udon is delicious. In both sentences, udon is the subject in both grammatical and real senses.

Summary of Short-Forms

At the end of the discussion about the short-forms, there is a table in which all short-form conjugational endings are included. They are the dictionary form, present tense affirmative, present tense negative, past tense affirmative and past tense negative of three kinds of verbs, two kinds of adjectives and nouns. These endings called suffix or inflection by grammarians determine the tenses and aspects. In this case, the romaji only is used without Hiragana, in order to split one syllable in half for u-verbs when the stem and suffix are separated. Also, u-verbs often include an infix or middle part besides the stem. When an infix is included, it will be added before the suffix in the table. See the following:

Endings of All Short-Forms

	Dictionary Form	Present Affirmative	Present Negative	Past Affirmative	Past Negative
I-Adjectives	-i	-i	- kunai	-katta	- kunakatta
Na-adjectives/ nouns	-na	- da	- janai	- datta	- janakatta
U-verbs	-u	-u	-i-nai	Same as Te-form except last vowel	-a-nakatta
Ru-verbs	-ru	-ru	-nai	-ta	-nakatta
Irregular Verbs	-ru	-ru	-nai	-ta	-nakatta

Just like long (standard) forms, na-adjectives and nouns of the short-forms act exactly in the same way. Also, ru-verbs and irregular verbs have the same endings, since their irregularity lies only in their stem change. The past tense affirmative of u-verbs takes various forms, nearly identical with te-form except the last vowel.

Masho & Masho ka Ending for Suggestions

At the end of this chapterましょう (masho) and ましょうか (masho ka) ending of verbs with two-fold usages will be introduced.

The first way of using this expression is to suggest a plan of action. For instance, a statement 晩御飯をたべましょう (bangohan o tabe-masho) may be translated, "Let's eat supper". In this context, the speaker is suggesting to the person being addressed to eat supper. The second way of using this expression is offering assistance to the person being addressed and "masho" in this context may be translated as "let me do". "Masho" and "masho ka" endings have nearly identical meanings and both of them are used in the context to suggest a plan of action together, and to offer assistance to the addressee. However, "masho ka" sounds a little softer and giving the addressee more room to decide whether he or she accepts or declines your offer. On the other hand, "masho" without the final "ka" sounds more forceful. The following two examples include masho-forms in two different contexts:

a) 浅草でどじょうを食べましょうか。(Asakusa de dojo o tabe-masho ka). "shall we eat dojo fish (louch) in Asakusa"?

b) 昼御飯を作りましょうか。(Hirugohan o tsukuri-masho ka). "Shall I make lunch"?

In the first sentence, you are suggesting to your addressee to eat loach fish in the Asakusa district of Tokyo. On the other hand, in the second sentence, you are suggesting to prepare and serve lunch to someone else. (Dojo Loach - p. 185)

NOTES

6

INTERMEDIATE JAPANESE GRAMMAR

General Overview

This chapter will review several items for intermediate level Japanese grammar that includes verb ending sentences such as verb (present tense short-forms) + つもりです (tsumori desu), verb stem + たいです (tai desu), verb (past tense short-forms) + 事があります (koto ga arimasu). "Tsumori desu" expressions demonstrate one's intention and "tai desu" demonstrate his or her desires to do or not to do certain things. "Koto ga arimasu" has nearly the equivalent meaning as the present perfect tense in English, and demonstrates a past experience. Other expressions are ほうがいいです (hoogaii-desu), the ending for advice giving, すぎます (sugi-masu), the ending to tell excessiveness, andんです (n-desu), the ending to explain reasons.

Another area to be covered will be adjective and noun ending sentences with the adjective/noun + なる (naru) ending that means "becoming". The "rareru" ending is for potential and super-polite expressions.

Tsumori Ending (Plans & Intentions)

First of all, the つもり (tsumori) ending indicates the intention of the speaker to do or not to do in future. It follows verbs in the present tense short forms in both the affirmative and negative and tells activities that a person plans to carry out. The tables underneath will tell you "tsumori" endings in both standard and short-forms which come after the short-form present tense.

Tsumori Endings (Standard-Forms)

Standard form present tense affirmative (desu ending)	Standard form present tense negative (ja nai-desu ending)	Standard form past tense affirmative (deshita ending)	Standard form past tense negative (ja-nakkatta-desu ending)
つもりです tsumori-desu	つもりじゃないです tsumori-ja-nai-desu	つもりでした tsumori-deshita	つもりじゃなかったです tsumori-ja-akatta-desu

Tsumori Endings (Short-Forms)

Short-form present tense affirmative (da ending)	Short-form present tense negative (ja nai ending)	Short-form past tense affirmative (datta ending)	Short-form past tense negative (ja nakatta ending)
つもりだ tsumori-da	つもりじゃない tsumori-ja-nai	つもりだった tsumori-datta	つもりじゃなかった tsumori-ja-nakatta

The examples of sentences which include the present tense affirmative and negative of "tsumori-desu" endings are as follows: a) ロバートさんはあした名古屋でうどんを食べるつもりです。 (Robaato san wa ashita Nagoya de udon o taberu tsumori-desu). "Robert intends to eat udon in Nagoya tomorrow" b) メアリーさんは来週大阪で映画を見るつもりじゃないです。 (Mearii san wa raishuu Osaka de eega o miru tsumori-ja-nai-desu) "Mary does not intend to watch a movie in Osaka next week".

In both sentences above, the short-form verb before the "tsumori" is affirmative. It is also possible to make the verb prior to tsumori negative. At the same time, both the pre-tsumori verb and tsumori ending can be negative, since double negatives are commonly used in the Japanese language. Examples are as follows:

a) けんさんは土曜日に図書館で勉強しないつもりです。 (Ken san wa doyoobi ni toshokande benkyoo shinai tsumori-desu). "Ken does not intend to study in the library on Saturday" b) みちこさんは来週京都で買い物をしないつもりじゃないです。 (Michiko san wa raishuu Kyoto de kaimono o shinai tsumori-ja-nai-desu) "Mary does not "un-intend" to watch a movie in Osaka next week".

The first sentence is an example that only the pre-tsumori short-form verb is negative and the tsumori ending is affirmative. The second sentence is an example of a typical double negative expression in Japanese in which both pre-tsumori short-form verb and tsumori ending are negative. There is no way to translate this Japanese double negative other than the description "non-intend". Double negatives in Japanese produce an affirmative sense like many other languages including Standard English, while doubled negatives intensify the negation. At the same time, double negatives in Japanese express the positive implications in a more subtle and covert way than a simple affirmative.

With respect to the past tense of "tsumori" ending, keep in mind that since the pre-tsumori short-form verb is always present tense, the past tense of tsumori ending always indicates the simple past. The past tense of "tsumori" endings describes the intentions or plans that the speaker conceived in his or her mind in the past. Unlike the complex sentences which include the pattern Subject + Adjectives (short form) + と(to) +言っていました/言っていた (itte-imashita/itte-ita), or Subject + Verbs (short form) or Subject + Adjectives (short form) + と(to) +思います/思う(omoimasu/omou), tsumori ending sentences never describe events in a "past of the past".

a) ロバートさんはあした東京で軍鶏を食べるつもりでした。(Robaato san wa ashita Tokyo de shamo o taberu tsumori-deshita). "Robert intended to eat shamo chicken in Tokyo tomorrow" b) メアリーさんは明日大阪で歌舞伎を見るつもりじゃなかったです。(Mearii san wa ashita Osaka de Kabuki o miru tsumori-ja-nakatta-desu) "Mary didn't intend to watch Kabuki in Osaka tomorrow" c) けんさんは日曜日に喫茶店で勉強しないつもりでした。(Ken san wa nichiyoobi ni kissaten de benkyoo shinai tsumori-deshita). "Ken did not intend to study in a coffee shop on Saturday" d) みちこさんは来週名古屋で焼酎を飲まないつもりじゃなかったです。(Michiko san wa raishuu Nagoya de shochu o nomanai tsumori-ja-nakatta-desu) "Mary did not "un-intend" to drink shochu (Japanese vodka) in Nagoya next week". (Shamo Chick - p. 187/Kabuki - p. 194)

In the first two sentences, the short-form verb before the "tsumori" is affirmative. The very first sentence is an example of both the pre-tsumori short-form and tsumori ending as affirmative. The entire sentence is past tense affirmative, since the tsumori ending is affirmative past tense. In the second sentence, the entire sentence is past tense negative since the tsumori ending is the past form negative. In the third sentence, the pre-tsumori short-form verb is negative, but the tsumori ending is affirmative. Both second and third sentences have simply negative indications and these two usages are interchangeable and nearly identical. The fourth sentence is a somewhat strange double negative with a positive implication in a more subtle and covert way than a simple affirmative.

Tai desu (Wishes & desires)

To express a desire, hope, aspiration and wishes to do certain things follows the format verb stem + たいです (tai desu), the verb stem + tai desu ending follows either Noun + ga or Noun + o. If it is Noun + ga + tai desu, the noun is treated as the subject of the sentence. If you say that (Ramen ga tabetai desu) "I want to eat ramen (noodle), "ramen" is the subject of the sentence instead of the person who eats it. You may translate, "Ramen is desirable to eat for me". On the other hand, if you state a sentence (Ramen o tabetai desu), the speaker who wants to eat "ramen" is the subject of the sentence, though the meaning of the sentence is exactly identical to the previous sentence. The following tables show verb stem and "tai-desu" endings in both standard and short-forms which come after the short-form present tense. The first table is for the standard (long) form conjugation of the verb stem + たいです (tai desu) endings:

Tai Endings (Standard-Forms)

	Standard form present tense affirmative	Standard form present tense negative	Standard form past tense affirmative	Standard form past tense negative
u-verbs のむ (nomu) to drink	のみ-たいです nom-i-tai-desu	のみ-たくないです nom-i-takunai-desu	のみ-たかったです nom-i-takatta-desu	のみ-たくなかったです nom-i-takunakatta-desu
ru-verbs たべる (tabe-ru) to eat	たべたいです tabe-tai-desu	たべたくないです tabe-takunai-desu	たべたかったです tabe-takatta-desu	たべたくなかったです tabe-takunakatta-desu
irregular verb くる (ku-ru) to come	き-たいです ki-tai-desu	き-たくないです ki-takunai-desu	き-たかったです ki-takatta-desu	き-たくなかったです ki-takunakatta-desu
irregular verb する (su-ru) to do	し-たいです shi-tai-desu	し-たくないです shi-takunai-desu	し-たかったです shi-takatta-desu	し-たくなかったです shi-takunakatta-desu

When the present tense affirmative of masu-form is created, you must take off the last vowel "u" and keep the consonant "m". After removing "u", you need to add an infix or middle part "i", and then add "masu". For ru-verbs, you simply have to drop the last syllable "ru" and add "tai-desu. Regarding irregular verbs (kuru and suru), the process is exactly the same as ru-verbs, except for minor stem changes. For "kuru", the vowel "u" after the consonant "k" turns into "i", and for suru, the vowel "u" after the consonant "s" turns into "i" and add another consonant "h" after "s". The formation of the verb stem + たいです (tai desu) endings require exactly the same process as creating masu-form from the dictionary form. Following are examples of short-forms of "taidesu" endings of these verbs:

Tai Endings (Short-Forms)

	Short-form present tense affirmative	Short-form present tense negative	Short-form past tense affirmative	Short-form past tense negative
u-verbs のむ (nomu) to drink	のm-i-たい nom-i-tai	のm-i-たくない nom-i-takunai	のm-i-たかった nom-i-takatta	のm-i-たくなかった nom-i-takunakatta
ru-verbs たべる (tabe-ru) to eat	たべ-たい tabe-tai	たべ-たくない tabe-takunai	たべ-たかった tabe-takatta	たべ-たくなかった tabe-takunakatta
irregular verb くる (ku-ru) to come	き-たい ki-tai	き-たくない ki-takunai	き-たかった ki-takatta	き-たくなかった ki-takunakatta
irregular verb する (su-ru) to do	し-たい shi-tai	し-たくない shi-takunai	し-たかった shi-takatta	し-たくなかった shi-takunakatta

The short-forms of "taidesu" endings are the same format as the i-adjectives, and "ta-i", "ta-kunai", "ta-katta" and "ta-ku-nakatta" endings. Also, for u-verbs, you need to drop the final vowel "u" and add the infix "i" before the suffix "ta-kunai" "ta-katta" and "ta-ku-nakatta" respectively in the same way as the masu-forms.

Ta Koto ga arimasu (past experience)

Next, the short-form past tense + ことがあります (koto ga arimasu) describes your past experience and has nearly the equivalent implication as the present perfect tense in English. In this expression, the short-form verb before "koto ga arimasu" is always past tense, but "arimasu" ending at the very end of the sentence is either present or past tense. However, holding negatives in both short-form endings and "arimasu" endings at the end does not indicate "past of past" just like complex sentences with "to omoimasu" or "to itte-imashita" endings. Examples of "koto ga arimasu" sentences are the following:

a) ロバートさんは広島でお好み焼きを食べたことがあります。(Robaato san wa Hiroshima de okonomiyaki o tabeta kotoga-arimasu). "Robert has eaten Okonomiyaki in Hiroshima"

b) メアリーさんは大吟醸酒を飲んだことがありません。(Mearii san wa daiginjo-shu o nonda kotoga-arimasen) "Mary has not tasted daiginjyo sake".

N-desu (explanation mode)

Next, the short-form present or past tense of verbs, adjectives and nouns + んです (n desu) explains the situation or circumstance that you are in. In Japanese there are two different ways of making a statement. One is simply stating a fact that you have observed using plain present or past tense. For instance, a sentence 電車が来ませんでした (Densha ga kimasen deshita) simply indicates the fact that "The train did not come". In English, there is nothing beyond this level of statement or any way of making expressions which imply the consequence that the train did not come. However, Japanese has an alternative way of making a statement which might offer an explanation for a certain circumstance or condition. An alternative expression with the same content 電車が来なかったんです (Densha ga ko-nakatta-n-desu) might provide a reason that you did not show up to an appointment or come to a meeting late.

The "n-desu" ending follows the short form verbs, adjectives and nouns. The short-form predicate can be either in the affirmative or negative or either in the present tense or past tense. Nevertheless, the n-desu ending per se does not usually appear in the past tense or in the negative. However, it can take either in the long (standard) forms or the short-forms. When it is in the short-forms, the sentence ends in んだ "n-da" instead of "n-desu". Following are explanation mode endings of the following verbs adjectives and a noun:

N-desu Endings (Explamation Mode)

	Dictionary Form	Report Sentences (present tense)	んです(n-desu) form (affirmative present tense)	んです(n-desu) form (affirmative past tense)	んです (n-desu) form (negative present tense)	んです (n-desu) form (negative past tense)
U-verbs	飲む (nomu) "drink"	飲みます	飲むんです (nomu-n-desu)	飲んだんです (nonda-n-desu)	飲まないんです (nom-a-nai-n-desu)	飲まなかったんです (nom-a-nakatta-n-desu)
Ru-verbs	食べる (taberu) "eat"	食べます	食べるんです (taberu-n-desu)	食べたんです (tabeta-n-desu)	食べないんです (tabe-nai-n-desu)	食べなかったんです (tabe-nakatta-n-desu)
I-adjectives	おいしい (oishii) "delicious"	おいしいです (oishii- desu)	おいしいんです (oishi-n-desu)	おいしかったんです (oishikatta-n-desu)	おいしくないんです (oishiku-nai-n-desu)	おいしくなかったんです (oishiku-nakatta-n-desu)
Na-adjectives	しずかな (shizuka-na) "quiet"	しずかです (shizuka-desu)	しずかなんです (shizuka-na-n-desu)	しずかだったんです (shizuka-datta-n-desu)	しずかじゃないんです (shizika-ja-nai-n-desu)	しずかじゃなかったんです (shizika-ja-nakatta-n-desu)
Nouns	学生 (gakusee) "student"	学生です (gakusee-desu)	学生なんです (gakusee-na-n-desu)	学生だったんです (gakusee-datta-n-desu)	学生じゃないんです (gakusee-janai-n-desu)	学生じゃなかったんです (gakusee-janakatta-n-desu)

The following five sentences are examples with the "n-desu" ending that explains certain situations or circumstances.

a) ロバートさんは明日東京でともだちと軍鶏を食べるんです。(Robaato san wa ashita Tokyo de tomodachi to shamo o taberu-n-desu). "Robert eats shamo chicken with his friends in Tokyo tomorrow, (and it's why he must be there)" b) メアリーさんは昨日家で勉強しなかったんです。(Mearii san wa kinoo ie de benkyoo-shi-nakatta-n-desu) "Mary didn't study at home yesterday, (and it is why she didn't do well in her exam)" c) たけしさんは先週の金曜日に頭が痛かったんです。(Takeshi san wa senshuu no kinyoobi ni atamaga itakatta-n-desu). "Takeshi had headache on last Friday (and it explains why he missed class then)" d) 大勝軒のラーメンはとても美味しいんです。(Taishoken no raamen wa totemo oishii-n-desu) "Taishoken Restaurant's Ramen noodle is very delicious, (and it is why I go there everyday)". e) みちこさんはてんぷらそばがだいすきなんです。(Michiko san wa Tempura Soba ga daisukina-n-desu) "Michiko likes soba noodle with Tempura very much, (and it is why she eats it everyday)".

The first and second sentences are examples of verbal short-form (affirmative and negative) + "n-desu" ending. The third and forth sentences are examples of i-adjective (present and past tenses) and "n-desu" ending. The fourth sentence is an example of na-adjective (present tense) and "n-desu" ending. In na-adjective present tense, the final "na" in the dictionary form is retained. However, in the negative, the verb before "n-desu" ending is だった (data), simply a short form past tense of na-adjectives.

Sugiru (Too much)

The verb or adjective stem + すぎる (sugiru) expression indicates that something is "too much" or "to excess". The ending of すぎる (sugiru) conjugates as a regular ru-verb. Following are examples of the conjugation pattern of predicates which include "sugi-masu" endings and the stem of u-verbs, ru-verbs, adjectives:

Sugiru Too Much

	Dictionary Form	Report Sentences (present tense)	すぎる (sugiru) form (present tense)	すぎる (sugiru) form (past tense)
U-verbs	のむ (nom-u) "drink"	のみます (nom-i-masu)	のみすぎます (nom-i-sugi-masu)	のみすぎました (nom-i-sugi-mashita)
Ru-verbs	たべる (tabe-ru) "eat"	たべます (tabe-masu)	たべすぎます (tabe-sugi-masu)	たべすぎました (tabe-sugi-mashita)
I-adjectives	たかい (takai) "expensive"	たかいです (takai-desu)	たかすぎます (taka-sugi-masu)	たかすぎました (taka-sugi-mashita
Na-adjectives	しずか-な (shizuka-na) "quiet"	しずかです (shizuka-desu)	しずかすぎます (shizuka-sugimasu)	しずかすぎました (shizuka-sugi-mashita)

For u-verbs, the suffix "u" is dropped from the dictionary form and an infix "i" is added before the "sugi-masu"ending. Otherwise, simply add "sugi-masu" endings to the end of the stems of ru-verbs, "i" and "na" adjectives and nouns. If the "sugiru" ending has short-form, the present tense affirmative and negative are "sugiru" and "suginai". The past tense affirmative and negative are "sugita" and "suginakatta". The "Sugiru" ending conjugates exactly in the same way as a ru-verb. If "sugiru" stands alone and acts independently, it is a ru-verb which means to go to excess or pass the boundary.

Following shows the long and short-forms, and present and past tenses of the verb "sugiru" which is used as the very end of the "sugi-masu" expression:

Sugiru Ending Conjugation

Dictionary form	すぎる (sugi-ru)
Long form present affirmative	すぎます (sugi-masu)
Long form present negative	すぎません (sugi-masenn)
Long form past affirmative	すぎました (sugi-mashita)
Long form past negative	すぎませんでした (sugi-endeshita)
Short-form present affirmative	すぎる (sugi-ru)
Short form present negative	すぎない (sugi-nai)
Short-form past affirmative	すぎた (sugi-ta)
Short-form past negative	すぎなかった (sigi-i-nakata)

Following are sample sentences which include "sugiru" endings that indicate something is "too much" or "to excess":

a) けんさんは忘年会で焼酎を飲みすぎました。(Ken san wa Bōnenkai de shochu o nomi-sugi-mashita). "Ken drunk too much shochu in Bōnenkai (Forget-the-year Parties)"[77] b) メアリーさんは新年会でお餅を食べすぎました。(Mearii san wa Shinnenkai de Omochi o tabe-sigi-mashita) "Mary ate Mochi (rice cake) too much in the New Year Parties" c) １２月の街はにぎやかすぎます。(Jyuunigatsu no machi wa nigiyaka-sugimasu). "December's town (town during December) is too lively" d) 東京の50辛カレーは辛すぎます。(Tokyo no gojukkara karee wa kara-sugi-masu) "Fifty times spice curry in Tokyo is too spicy". (Bonenkai - p. 195/Spicy Curry - p.191)

The first and second sentences include verb + sugiru (long-form past tense) endings. The third and fourth sentences end in na-adjective and i-adjective with sugiru (long-form present) respectively.

Potential Form

The potential form with verb stem + "e-ru" or "rareru" ending indicate one's ability and potential to do certain things. The "e-ru" ending is applied to u-verbs and "rareru" ending to ru-verbs and irregular verb "kuru" respectively. For the potential forms, there is a minor difference between u-verbs and ru-verbs just like all other conjugational patterns. Among irregular verbs, "kuru" behaves in a similar way as ru-verbs just as almost all other conjugation patterns. However, "suru" acts in a completely different way. The following table shows potential forms of each sample of u-verbs, ru-verbs and a couple of irregular verbs.

---

77 Bōnenkai (忘年会) or "Forget-the-year Parties" take place throughout December while Shinnenkai (新年会) or "New Year Parties" take place in January. Many Japanese drink and eat excessively in both Bōnenkai and Shinnenkai.

Potential Verbs (Short-Forms)

	Dictionary Form	Present Short Affirmative	Present Short Negative	Past Short Affirmative	Past Short Negative
U-Verbs	はなす hanas-u (speak)	はなせる hanas-e-ru	はなせない hanas-e-nai	はなせた hanas-e-ta	はなせなかった hanas-e-nakatta
Ru-verbs	見る mi-ru (see)	見られる mi-rareru	見られない mi-rarenai	見られた mi-rareta	見られなかった mi-rarenakatta
Irregular Verbs	来る ku-ru (come)	来られる ko-rareru	来られない ko-rarenai	来られた ko-rareta	来られなかった ko-rarenakatta
	する su-ru (do)	できる deki-ru	できない deki-nai	できた deki-ta	できなかった deki-nakatta

For the potential forms, u-verbs drop the final "u" from the dictionary form and add "eru", "enai", "eta" and "enakatta" respectively. Ru-verbs, on the other hand, drop the final "ru" and add "rareru", "rarenai", "rareta" and "rarenakatta" respectively. "Kuru" acts in the same way as ru-verbs except the vowel after "k" in the stem turns into "o" from "u" just like all other conjugational forms. However, "suru" in this case has a drastic irregularity just like English irregular verbs. In fact, できる (dekiru) was originally a different verb with no connection with "suru". When "dekiru" stands alone, it is a ru-verb which means to complete or be capable of doing something. In the English vocabulary, it has a close parallel with "went", the past tense of the verb "to go". In Old English, "went" was the past tense of another verb "wend" and had no relationship with "go". Later, it started to be used as the past tense of "go" as "wend" became obsolete. Likewise, it is easy to assume that people started using "dekiru" as the potential form of "suru" sometime in the past.

Following are some sample sentences which include potential forms:

a) けんさんは英語と中国語が話せます。 (Ken san wa eego to chuugokugo ga hanase-masu). "Ken can speak English and Chinese languages" b) 今晩は六本木ヒルズから東京タワーのライトアップが見られます。 (Konban wa Roppongi-hiruzu kara Tokyo Tawaa no raito-appu ga mirare-masu) "Tonight, you can see the light-up of Tokyo Tower from Roppongi Hills" c) 山下さんは明日の会議に来られません。 (Yamashita san wa ashita no kaigi ni korare-masen). "Yamashita will not be able to come to the meeting tomorrow" d) メアリーさんはバスケットボールが出来ません。 (Mearii san wa basuketto-booru ga deki-masen) "Mary cannot do (play) basketball".

The first and second sentences are potential form affirmatives with a u-verb and ru-verb respectively. The third and fourth ones include the potential form negatives of "kuru" and "suru". Regarding the fourth sentence, the predicate has an appearance to be the present tense negative of "dekiru" a ru-verb which means to "complete" or "capable to do", instead of the potential form of some other verb.

There are shorter alternative potential forms of ru-verb and the irregular verb 来る (kuru). They are called ら抜き言葉 (ranuki kotoba) or "ra-less expressions" for the potential forms. They have similar endings to the potential forms of u-verbs which are made by adding the suffix "reru" instead of "rareru", previously considered ungrammatical expressions. However, the "reru" alternative for the ru-verbs obtained public acceptance during the past two decades. Younger people in the third millennium use "reru" alternative more often than more orthodox and traditional "rareru" expressions of the potential expressions of ru-verbs. The following table displays *ra*-less potential forms ru-verbs and the irregular verb "kuru":

Potential Verbs (With Ra-less Alternatives)

	Dictionary Forms	Standard Potential Forms	Ra-less Potential Forms
Ru-verbs	見る mi-ru (see)	見られる mi-rareru	見れる mi-reru
	食べる tabe-ru (see)	食べられる tabe-rareru	食べれる tabe-reru
Irregular Verb	来る ku-ru (come)	来られる ko-rareru	来れる ko-reru

Passive Voice

The passive voice with verb stem + "a-reru" or "rareru" ending indicate one's ability and potential to do certain things. The passive voice is antithetical to "ranuki kotoba" of the potential forms, since "ra" is added to both u-verbs and ru-verbs. The passive voice is usually used to express complaint or dissatisfaction when one in inconvenienced by something someone else has done. The examples of the passive voice verbs are in the following table.

For the passive voice, u-verbs have "areru" endings that are very similar to re-verbs instead of "eru" ending. Regarding ru-verbs and the irregular verb "kuru", the passive voice is identical to the potential forms. For another irregular verb "suru", there is no drastic irregularity as in the potential form, but the vowel of the stem is simply shifted from "u" to "a". The sentence structure is Subject + Agent of Action + に (ni) + Direct Object + を (o) + Passive Voice Verb. The subject is often omitted just as in many Japanese sentences, and the direct object is present only with transitive verbs.

The following sentences are examples which include the passive voice:

a) けんさんはとなりのビルからホテルの部屋を見られました。(Ken san wa tonari no biru kara hoteru no heya o mirare-mashita) "Ken's hotel room was seen by someone from the next building" b) ロバートさんはどろぼうに新しいカメラを取られました。(Robaato san wa doroboo ni atarashii kamera o torare-mashita). "Robert had his new camera stolen by a thief" c) メアリーさんはともだちに手紙を読まれました。(Mearii san wa tomodachi ni tegami o yomare-mashita) "Mary had her letter read by her friend" d) たけしさんは忘年会で酒に飲まれました。(Takeshi san wa boonenkai de sake ni nomare-mashita). "Takeshi was very drunk in the Bonenkai Party".

The passive voice usually indicates a person is inconvenienced or given troubles by someone else[78]. In the second sentence, "torareru", or being taken, is nearly a synonym of 盗まれる (nusumareru) or being stolen, in a certain context. The expression "sake ni nomareru" or being drunk, in the fourth sentence, is a very unique idiomatic expression. Literally, sake or alcohol is an agent that drinks people instead of having them drink it. When sake drinks people, it makes them out of control, irresponsible and obnoxious.

Passive Voice (Short-Forms)

	Dictionary Form	Present Short Affirmative	Present Short Negative	Past Short Affirmative	Past Short Negative
U-Verbs	飲む nom-u (Drink)	飲まれる nom-a-reru	飲まれない nom-a-renai	飲まれた nom-a-reta	飲まれなかった nom-a-renakatta
Ru-verbs	見る mi-ru (see)	見られる mi-rareru	見られない mi-rarenai	見られた mi-rareta	見られなかった mi-rarenakatta
Irregular Verbs	来る ku-ru (come)	来られる ko-rareru	来られない ko-rarenai	来られた ko-rareta	来られなかった ko-rarenakatta
	する su-ru (do)	される sare-ru	されない sare-nai	された sare-ta	されなかった sare-nakatta

---

78 Japanese big cities have many highrise hotels and office buildings, so that a peeping Tom may be hiding in one of these buildings and you'd better use the curtain.

Causative Forms

Causative forms with the verb stem + "a-seru" or "saseru" ending describe a person making or letting someone else do something. In order to convert the dictionary form into the causative form, ru-verbs drop the final "ru" and add "saseru" and u-verbs drop the final "u" and add "a-seru". The following table displays the conjugation of the causative forms of three different kind of verbs in the present and past tenses:

Causative Forms

	Dictionary Form	Present Short Affirmative	Present Short Negative	Past Short Affirmative	Past Short Negative
U-Verbs	死ぬ shin-u (die)	死なせる shin-a-seru	死なせない shin-a-senai	死なせた shin-a-s-eta	死なせなかった shin-as-enakatta
Ru-verbs	食べる taberu (eat)	食べさせる tabe-saseru	食べさせない tabe-sasenai	食べさせた tabe-saseta	食べさせなかった tabe-sasenakatta
Irregular Verbs	来る ku-ru (come)	来させる ko-saseru	来させない ko-sasenai	来させた ko-saseta	来させなかった ko-sasenakatta
	する su-ru (do)	させる saseru	させない sasenai	させた saseta	させなかった sasenakatta

"Shinaseru" or the causative form of "shinu" is either letting someone die or causing his or her death. In the former case, it might indicate that one simply observes someone else die either from a natural cause or some inevitable reason and does not interfere in the process of his or her death. If it is the latter case, one is criminally responsible for someone else's death and the simple active voice of another verb 殺す (korosu), which means to kill or murder is also applicable to this action. "Tabesaseru" is the causative form of "taberu" or, to eat, and may simply mean to let someone or make someone else to eat. However, it is also an idiomatic expression that indicates to feed, nurture or financially support someone.

Causative-Passive Forms

The causative form, which would combines させる (saseru) and られる (rareru) or a-れる (a-reru) together is a format used when forced to do or harassed to do something that you are reluctant to do. There are five different formats of making causative-passive forms. The first format is ru-verbs in which the final "ru" is dropped and added to make させられる (sase-rareru). For instance, the causative-passive form of "taberu" is 食べさせられる (tabe-sase-rareru), that is, being forced to eat something. The second format is u-verbs that end with "su" in the dictionary form. You need to drop the final "u" and add a-せられる (a-se-rareru). The third format belongs to all other u-verbs, and you need to drop the final "u" and add "a-sareru. The following sentences are examples of causative-passive forms:

a) メアリーさんは京都ですっぽんを食べさせられました。(Mearii san wa kyoto de suppon o tabe-sase-rare-mashita) "Mary was forced to eat suppon (soft-shell turtle) in Kyoto" b) トムさんはカラオケバーで歌を歌わせられました。(Tomu san wa Karaoke-baa de uta o utawase-rare-mashita). "Tom was made to sing in a Karaoke bar" c) ロバートさんはカラオケバーで下手な歌を聞かされました。(Robaato san wa Karaoke-baa de heta-na uta o kikasare-

mashita). "Robert was made to hear a clumsy song in a Karaoke bar"
d) たけしさんは図書館に本を返させられました。(Takeshi san wa
Toshokan ni hon o kaesase- rare-mashita). "Takeshi was forced to
return a book to the library".

[79]The first sentence includes the causative-passive of "taberu"
which means that someone is forced to eat some food item
reluctantly. The second and third sentences include causative-
passive forms of ordinary u-verbs. The second sentence includes the
causative-passive of "utau" which means that someone is forced
to sing. The third sentence includes the causative-passive of "kiku"
which means that someone is forced to hear.

"Karaoke", is an international entertainment that originated in
Japan. Etymologically, "karaoke" is a compound word of 空 (kara)
or "empty" and オケ (oke) or an abbreviated version of the English
word "orchestra", so that the word literally means "empty orchestra."
In a Karaoke machine, there are many different "empty tunes" in
which participants insert their own voice. Finally, the fourth sentence
includes the causative-passive forms of u-verbs that end with"su" in
the dictionary form. The verb "kaesu" took the form of the past tense
causative-passive "kaesase-rarere-mashita" which means "was forced
to return".

Honoring Others in Giving (Ageru & Kureru)

In Japanese, there are two different verbs for giving in two
different contexts. They are あげる (ageru) and くれる (kureru) and
both of them are ru-verbs. Japanese use these verbs depending on
the direction of the transaction. "Ageru" is used in the contexts: "I give
to you", "You give to others", "I give to others", and "Someone gives to

---

79   Most Westerners in Japan are reluctantant to eat any kind of reptiles at
     first. However, they often taste a small bit of suppon after being persistently
     persuaded to eat by a Japanese national. Then, many of them find it very tasty
     and decide to eat more. Strangely enough, some of them become hooked on the
     rare delicacy and visit a suppon restaurant repeatedly.

someone else". On the other hand, "kureru" are used in the contexts: "Someone gives me", "You give me", and "Someone gives you".

The former is used when the subject is the speaker himself or herself, and the latter is used in other contexts. "Ageru" originally stemmed from another verb 明ける (akeru) that literally means the sun goes up in the morning. It implies that an object goes up like a rising sun when it goes to the receipient. At the same time, "Kureru" literally means that the sun goes down and carries the implication that something goes down when it goes to the recipient. [80]Takehiro Kanaya maintains that both あげる (ageru) and くれる (kureru) stem from (yamato kotoba) or the Japanese language before the 7th Century in which Prince Shotoku opened up his country to Chinese influence. He also contrasted other synonymous verbs like 明ける (akeru) "to dawn" and 暮れる (kureru) "Sun goes down" and adjectives like 赤い (akai) "red" and 黒い (kuroi) "black", 明るい (akarui) "bright" and 暗い (kurai) "dark" and remarked that they all stem from the ancient language in the illiterate era. He also maintains that it has strong linkage with the Japanese mentality and value system which honors others and regard themselves lower than others. In the Confucian based value system in Japan, it is considered virtuous that one places others higher than himself or herself. It is debatable if the Japanese had a similar value system to place others in a higher position than himself or herself during pre-Confucian era before the 7th Century. In my personal view, "ageru" and "kureru" stemmed from the same origin, but were created after the era that the Confucian value system was imported from China.

On the other hand, もらう (morau), which means to receive or get, is more flexible and used in many different directions and relational contexts. However, with "morau" the speaker must identify himself or herself with the recipient of an object instead of the giver.

---

80   Takehiro Kanaya. Eego ni mo shugo ga nakatta [English also did not have the subject]. (Tokyo: Kodansha, 2004)

Therefore, it is wrong to say, あなたはわたしから手紙をもらいまし
た (Anata wa watashi kara tegami o morai-mashita), or "You received
a letter from me". In this context, you must use another verb 受け取
る (uketoru) with the same meaning so that the direction does not
matter.

7

Japanese Language & Anatomy of Writing System

This chapter reflects the basics of how I begin an introductory Japanese language course each September. I strongly emphasize the following characteristics of the language and require students to memorize them by the final exam of the first semester. They are: 1) Five vowels in modern Japanese , 2) All syllables end with vowels (open syllables) except ん, 3) No distinction between singular and plural for most nouns, 4) Use three different writing systems (hiragana, katakana and kanji).

These features summarize the distinctiveness of the language that beginners must be familiarized with at the beginning of the journey to learn a new language.

Origin

In the previous century, various theories came into existence to explain adequately the origin of the Japanese language, but nearly all of them failed. The number of these theories were numerous and they have become as varied as the seasons. Roy Andrew Miller (1924 – 2014), a very prolific writer and well-respected authority on this language recognized the uniqueness and enigma centered around its origin. He maintains that with respect to unraveling its ancestry,

Japanese is the only predominant language of a major nation that remains today without clarification of its origins.[81]

Today, most Western linguists believe it is related either to Korean, which is a geographic neighbor, or to the Ural-Altaic family, a language group which includes various languages in Asia and Europe, or to both. Like Japanese, Korean is an "orphan," and most advocates of Japanese-Altaic also propose that Korean belongs to its Altaic friends. The early formation of the Japanese language is unknown since Japan was an illiterate society until the 7th century.

Cang Jie & Origin of Kanji

Characters that Japan imported from the continent were called *kanji* (漢字) which referred to the Chinese characters used in Chinese, Japanese, Taiwanese and Korean writing systems. They were considered to have originated along the Yellow River in China, around 2000 BC. People in ancient East Asia used these characters with the rite of divination or magic, as cracks on burned bones were interpreted as real objects, giving a written representation of that object. Kanji were pictographs evolved from pictures or drawings of real physical objects just as the *sun* (日), the *moon* (月), a *tree* (木), a *horse* (馬), an *eye* (目), a *woman* (女), *fire* (火), and represented meanings instead of sounds. Today, most characters require a great deal of imagination to see the actual picture of what is represented. However, knowing the origin of the character and its evolution makes it much easier to understand the picture.

According to legend, the mystic Chinese emperor and legendary founder of the Chinese civilization was [82]*Huangdi* (黄帝) the Yellow Emperor, a cultural hero of ancient China. *Huangdi* had a minister

---

81   Roy Miller Origins of the Japanese Language: Lectures in Japan during the
      Academic Year 1977–78. (Seattle, USA: University of Washington Press, 1980).
82   Wikepedia: Yellow Emperor. Online at http://en.wikipedia.org/wiki/Huangdi

and official historian named [83]*Cang Jie* (蒼頡). [84]The legend said that Cang Jie invented a writing system, observing natural objects such as the imprints of bird steps on the ground. He paid close attention to the characteristics of all natural objects such as the sun, moon, stars, clouds, lakes and oceans, as well as every species of bird and beast. He began to create written characters according to the special characteristics of the objects he observed and compiled a long list of characters for writing. The God of Heaven was so impressed by this display of ingenuity that he caused grain to fall from the skies as a sign of his satisfaction with mankind. According to the legend, Cang Jie was portrayed possessing two pairs of eyes and four pupils, since he was an extraordinarily ingenious and insightful man who was capable of viewing present and future events.

Kokuji or Japanese made Kanji

Some kanji (漢字) or Chinese characters are classified as [85]*kokuji* (国字), that is, "national characters" that originated in Japan instead of China. Japanese reconstructed existing components of characters and created new characters with different meanings associated with the combination. They created several new combinations that did not exist in China. One example of kokuji is (働), which means to work. It is composed of *ninben* (亻) or person plus (動) or action.

Early Development of Writings & Literature

After the introduction of the Chinese characters, Japan eventually produced their own literature adapting the writing system to their own syntax and phonology. The earliest known literature written in Japanese was the [86]*Kojiki*[87] (古事記) (AD 712) and the *Manyoshu* (

---

83   Wikipedia: Cangjie. Online at http://en.wikipedia.org/wiki/Cangjie
84   Tatsuya Nagashima, ed. Nihon go kaiwa 30 shu II kyoshi shido yoko. [Teacher's Manual for Japanese in 30 weeks]. (Tokyo, Japan: PanaLinga Institute, 1982)
85   Wikipedia: Kanji. Online at http://en.wikipedia.org/wiki/Kanji
86   Wikipedia古事記. Online at http://ja.wikipedia.org/wiki/古事記
87   Wikipedia: Kojiki. Online at http://en.wikipedia.org/wiki/Kojiki

万葉集) (after AD 771). These works were valuable in revealing the evolution of the Japanese writing system from Chinese to a specialized system for recording spoken Japanese. The *Kojiki* largely maintains Chinese syntax, while using character combinations specific to Japanese for their semantic content. The *Manyoshu*, on the other hand, begins to use Chinese characters for their pronunciations to indicate Japanese words.

Around the 9th century, the Japanese created a writing system based on syllables: *Hiragana* and *katakana* (together: Kana). Of the two kana systems, hiragana is more cursive while katakana characters are quite angular. Both writers of *Kojik*i and *Manyoshu* used a rudimentary Kana system called [88]*manyogana*, which later developed into *Hiragana* and *katakana*. Japanese writings now consist of a liberal mixture of *kanji* and two sets of *Kana* systems that can be the most intimidating aspect of the language for new learners.

Hiragana and *katakana* are Japanese scripts and represent the sounds of syllables instead of the meanings. *Hiragana* and *katakana* each consist of 46 signs and have been strongly simplified over the centuries. These 46 characters are the first step in learning Japanese writing. When looking at a Japanese text, one can clearly distinguish between two kinds of signs: the complicated *kanji* and the simpler *kana* signs.

Among the syllables were five vowels あいうえお (a i u e o). The rest were syllables combined by one of these vowels with a consonant かきくけこらりる (ka ki ku ke ko ra ri ru ...). One exception was the ん (n), which consisted of the consonant only. In addition, they produce 23 voiced sounds like "g," "z," "d," "b" and "p" by adding two small strokes or a small circle in the top right corner next to some of the characters.

---

88   Wikipedia: Man'yōgana. Online at http://en.wikipedia.org/wiki/Manyogana

Hiragana text was made from Chinese character's *caoshuti* or a simplified form in the Heian era (794-1192). Since *hiragana* characters were developed and at first used mostly by women, so they were called *onna de*, which means "women's character." At the time, the Chinese writing system of *kanji* was considered too difficult for women, as it required years of study. In this era, a female writer, [89]*Murasaki Shikibu* (紫式部 – c.973–c.1014 or 1025), wrote [90]*Genji Monogarari* (源氏物語) or "story of Mr. Genji," in *hiragana*, one of the oldest long novels in the world.

While *hiragana* was called *onna de*, *katakana* was called *otoko de*, which meant "men's character." Even Japanese students of Buddhism (mostly priests or monks and predominantly males) were having trouble keeping up with the use of Chinese characters. It seemed that students taking notes during lectures often had a hard time with the pronunciations and meanings of the unfamiliar *kanji*. In order for them to be able to keep up with the pace of the lectures, phonetic shorthand had to be developed. Instead of adopting hiragana, another purely phonetic form of writing had to be developed. An interesting change in the method of deriving the characters was the use of only part of the Chinese character for simplification for writing quickly. They were called *katakana* (片仮名) or side-characters, since they took only one side of *kanji*. This new form of writing was also much more angular than *hiragana* because they were originally portions of *kanji* that were not cursive like *hiragana*. *Kibi no Makibi* (AD 693-755)[91], who spent over 20 years in China as a student, invented *katakana* through the simplification of a single element or radical from each of the phonetic kanji. Each *katakana* symbol

89   Wikepedia: Murasaki Shikibu. Online at http://en.wikipedia.org/wiki/
     Murasaki_Shikibu
90   Wikepedia: The Tale of Genji. Online at http://en.wikipedia.org/wiki/The_
     Tale_of_Genji
91   *Kibi no Makibi* went to China as a young man to study philosophy, history,
     politics, mathematics, astronomy, music, and military and stayed there for 19
     years, until he finally went back to Japan.

was derived from a Chinese character in the same way as each *Hiragana* symbol, except that the Hiragana were simplified from entire characters. *Katakana* were initially used only as pronunciation aids in Buddhist scriptures, but have been mixed with Chinese characters from the ninth century to the present.

The only question that remains is why the students didn't simply make use of *hiragana for notetaking*. Some have raised the question, "Were they afraid women would be able to read their notes?" At any rate, *katakana* began to be used in fields of science and learning.[92]

Hiragana & Katakana in Modern Japanese

[93]In modern times, hiragana and katakana have differentiated into distinct usages within written Japanese. Katakana is now used to write loan words, foreign words brought into Japanese, particularly those from the West after the 19th Century. Such borrowing usually occurred when the Japanese language lacked a native word to express a foreign idea.

In both Hiragana and Katakana, small や (ya), ゆ (yu), and よ (yo) are used to transcribe contracted sounds, and pronounced just like きゃ (kya), きゅ (kyu), and きょ (kyo) respectively. The small letter つ tsu is used to transcribe double consonants such as tt or pp. Examples are かった katta (won), ざっし zasshi (magazine) and はっぱ happa (leaf). A long e-vowel is usually transcribed by い instead of え. A long o-vowel is usually transcribed by う instead of お. For instance, "eega" (movie) is transcribed by えいが, and "tookyoo" (Tokyo) by とうきょう. The only difference between pronounciations of Hiragana and Katakana is that the long vowels are written with a hyphen or "–" in Katakana, but not in Hiragana. Examples are カー (kaa) "car", スキー(sukii) "ski" and ボール(booru) "ball".

---

92   Wikipedia: Kibi Makibi. (吉備真備) Online at http://en.wikipedia.org/wiki/Kibi_Makibi

93   Eri Banno, Ono, Yutaka, et al. Genki: An Integrated Course in elementary Japanese I, Vol. 1. Ibid.

Basic Greetings

With respect to basic greeting expressions in Japanese, the morning greeting is either おはよう (ohayoo) or おはようござい ます (ohayoo-gozaimasu). The first one is the shorter and more informal version, and the second one a more formal and respectful one. As stated previously, the Japanese language has a few different speech styles which are expected to be used in appropriate social settings. When you are addressing your family members and close friends, "ohayoo" is enough. However, when you greet your customers, supervisors or elderly people, you are expected to greet more respectfully, saying "ohayoo-gozaimasu". In the afternoon before it gets dark, the greeting is こんにちは (konnichiwa), and こんばん は (konbanwa) after sunset. In both expressions, the last character isは and pronounced "wa". The Hiragana character は is normally pronounced "ha" instead of "wa". However, when it is a particle coming after a noun which indicates the case, it is pronounced "wa". You might wonder why the character は following こんばん (konban) is a particle, since it is simply a greeting. However, both expressions "konnichiwa" and "konbanwa" used to be full sentences. Originally, "konnichi" meant "today" and "konban" meant "tonight". When the statements starting with "konnichi" and "konban" became customery greetings for the early afternoon and evening, they abbreviated all except the subject and the particle "wa".

When you see a person off, you must say さような ら (sayoonara), and おやすみ (oyasumi) or おやすみなさい (oyasuminasai) before going to bed. "Oyasumi" is the shorter and more informal version, and "oyasuminasai" the more formal and respectful one. When you want to say "Thank you" to someone, you must use the expression ありがとう (arigatoo) or ありがとうござ います (arigatoo-gozaimasu). The former is the shorter and more informal version, and the latter more formal and respectful. Next, すみ

ません (sumimasen) is an expression which means "Excuse me" or "I am sorry". If someone thinks he or she did something wrong to you, he or she might say "sumimasen". In response, you may say (iie) which means "no" or "not at all" to inform the person that you do not mind.

The following greetings are those which exist only in Japanese and possibly Korean, but not in any other language. When you leave your home, you must inform your family members that you are leaving, saying いってきます (ittekimasu). When you arrive home, you must say ただいま (tadaima) to inform you are back. At the same time, you must address いってらっしゃい (itterasshai) to a member of your household when he or she is leaving home, and say おかえりなさい (okaeri-nasai) when this person returns.

When you have a meal with your family or anyone else, you are expected to say いただきます (itadakimasu) and ごちそうさま (gochisoosama) when finishing. Both expressions indicate appreciation to a person who has prepared the meal. At the same time, the statement いただきます (itadakimasu) was originally a full sentence, 命をいただきます (inochi o itadakimasu) which means "I will take your life". It indicates an appreciation to creatures or plants that lost their lives to become your meal. It carries a concept that we must take lives of animals or plants to feed ourselves and survive. Saying "itadakimasu" constantly before each meal reminds us of this truth and makes us humble and respectful to God's creation.

Grammar & Syntax

The grammar of the Japanese language is very different from Indo European family languages including English, but is similar in some ways to Korean. It is also significantly different from Chinese except in writing. One of the well known characteristics of Japanese language may be the position of the verbs, copulas or predicates. They all come at the end of sentences, except in the case of a sentence's final particles like "ka", "ne" and "yo". An example of a simple sentence is "私は学生です" (Watashi wa gakusee desu), which means "I am a student". "Watashi" means "I" or first person singular and is the subject of this sentence. "Gakusee" means "student" and comes right after the subject. Finally, "desu" is the copula or the equivalent of "be" in English. In Japanese, it is also common to omit a subject when it is clear to the listener to what or to whom speaker is referring. Therefore, it is acceptable to say, "学生です" (gakusee desu), if the listener knows the context of the conversation. For instance, if a person is asked for his or her vocation, it is very obvious to whom this person is referring. In the same way, Japanese often omit direct objects or any other nouns whenever they think these nouns are unnecessary so as to make statements as brief and simple as possible.

Also, Japanese has no equivalency to articles like "a" or "the" coming in front of nouns. There is also no item which corresponds to the plural "s" at the end because there is no distinction between noun singular and plural. You must find out whether a noun like "gakusee" (student) is singular or plural based on the context. Sometimes, nouns for people and animals are followed by たち (tachi) which make them plural. However, most nouns for inanimate objects have nothing to indicate their plurality.[94]

Another unique component is "particles" which include two categories. One is "sentence final particles" and the other is "case indicating particles". The former is used for a formation of questions, confirmations and a short authoritative statement. An example of a sentence final particle is "ka" which makes an entire sentence interrogative. The latter comes after nouns and determines cases of nouns. Examples of these particles are "wa" or "ga" after the subject and "o" after the direct object. The proper use of the latter is an infamous and very annoying factor of Japanese for many learners,

94   Eri Banno, Ono, Yutaka, et al. Genki: An Integrated Course in elementary Japanese I, Vol. 1. Ibid.

particularly from the western hemisphere, since the rules are very versatile and can be confusing.

[95]Tatsuya Nagashima (1930 - 2006), a forerunner of Japanese language education, maintains that "particles" are the hardest components for Japanese language learners, since equivalent or similar components do not exist in many mother tongues. Nagashima, who developed his own textbooks in the 1980s to 1990s, asked his students, "What is the most difficult part of the Japanese language?" They responded that the use of particles is the most troublesome and overwhelmingly difficult.

In this chapter, I am going to introduce four of the cases indicating the particles は "wa", が "ga" , の "no", and を "o" as well as か "ka", ね "ne" and よ "yo", three of sentence final particles. First, I will discuss "wa" and "ga" coming after the subject and the difference between them. [96]Generally speaking, "wa" is classified as "topic particle" in Japanese textbooks, while "ga" is treated as a mere case indicator. In fact, "wa" indicates that the subject of the sentence is the "topic" to be discussed, while "ga" suggests that the subject is simply the subject. The following two sentences have practically identical meanings:

a) 私[97]はたけしです。 (Watashi <u>wa</u> Takeshi desu) "I am Takeshi".
b) 私がたけしです。 (Watashi <u>ga</u> Taakeshi desu) "I am Takeshi".

There is no doubt that both sentences have the same meaning and that the English translation is "I am Takeshi". However, these two are used in different circumstances. Sentence a) is a simple statement that the speaker's name is Takeshi and he is probably introducing himself to a stranger. In this circumstance, there is a

95   Tatsuya Nagashima, Grammatica Japonica. (Tokyo, Japan: PanaLinga Institute, 1996)
96   Eri Banno, Ono, Yutaka, et al. Genki: An Integrated Course in elementary Japanese I, Vol. 1. Ibid.
97   Normally, "は" is pronounced "ha", however it is uttered "wa" only when used as a particle.

person in question, but no one knows his name. What matters then in this situation is "who" that person is or what kind of identity this person has. Then, the problem is solved when he introduces himself as "Takeshi". However, the situation for the second sentence is a little different. The individual with the name "Takeshi" is responding to an inquiry that he is the one with this name. For example, a person named Takeshi may have forgotten something very important like his wallet, credit card or passport. It was urgent that someone named Takeshi is identified and so an announcement is made that they are looking for him. Then, someone shows up and introduces himself "私がたけしです." (Watashi ga Taakeshi desu). In this circumstance, the problem is solved when they find a person named "Takeshi".

Next, "no" is a possessive particle to connect two nouns and is extremely versatile. It is generally considered that the English equivalency of "no" is "of". However, that is not always correct. First, the syntax of "no" is opposite to "of", since the main idea comes after "no". For instance, a statement "a student of computers" is "コンピューターの学生" (konpyuutaa no gakusee), and word order is reversed. The closer English equivalency may be apostrophe + "s" instead of "of", and "computer's student" is better than "a student of computers". Also, "no" may be translated into "in", "on", or "at" depending on the context. For instance, "日本の大学" (Nihon no daigaku) is "a university in Japan"instead of "a university of Japan".

The particle "o" comes after the direct object. Examples of direct objects are food, drink, music, book, movie, etc. After direct "object + o", you must add a transitive verb to eat, drink, listen or read.

For instance, you may make a sentence "[98]私はすしをたべます[99]" (Watashi wa sushi o tabemasu) "I eat sushi","watashi" is

---

[98] The character は is normally pronounced "ha" instead of "wa". However, when it is a particle coming after a noun and indicate the case, it is pronounced "wa".

[99] The character for the particle "o" is "を" instead of "お" which is commonly used for the vowel "o" It is safe to conclude that the letter "を" is used exclusively for the case indicating particle after a direct object.

the subject and "wa" comes after the subject. "Sushi" is the direct object that comes after the subject and is followed by the particle "o". "Tabemasu" is the verb that comes at the end of a sentence in Japanese. It is also acceptable to omit the subject"Watashi" and particle "wa" if the context clearly communicates who is eating sushi. For instance, when a customer is going to order food in a restaurant, he or she may simply state "Sushi o tabemasu", because the waitress/waiter knows who is eating sushi.

Sentence final particles like "ka", "ne" and "yo" are placed at the very end of sentences. "Ka" forms questions when it is added after a verb or copula which usually comes at the end. For instance, the sentence, "たけしさんはすしをたべます" (Taakeshi san[100] wa sushi o tabemasu) simply means "Takeshi eats sushi". However, if "ka" is added after the verb "tabemasu," which means to eat, the sentence turns into an interrogative, "Does Takeshi eat sushi?"

"Ne" is placed when the speaker is seeking the listener's confirmation or agreement to what he or she has said. For instance, if you add "ne" to the end of a simple sentence, "たけしさんは日本人です" (Taakeshi san wa nihon jin desu) or "Takeshi is a Japanese person," it turns into a statement, "Takeshi Japanese person. Is it right?" It is not fully interrogative and the speaker has a weaker certainty. However, he or she does not have an absolute sureness to use a fully affirmative sentence and needs a confirmation from others.

"Yo" makes a statement more assertive and authoritative. For instance, a foreign traveler learns that "suppon" or soft shell turtle is one of the greatest delicacies in Japan. However, he is not sure if this information is true and asks a Japanese person about it. Then, this person loves "suppon" and wants to say it has fabulous taste with absolute certainty. He or she could say, "すっぽんはとてもおい

---

100 "さん" (san) is equivalent to English Mr. Mrs. or Miss and is added after person's name to pay respect to the person. It is gender neutral and may be placed with either a personal or family name.

しいですよ" (Suppon wa totemo oishii desu yo), or "Suppon is very delicious".

Like any other language, Japanese has verbs, adjectives, adverbs and other minor components. However, they act very differently from Indo European languages. Japanese has three kinds of verbs as well as two kinds of adjectives. Japanese verbs include u-verbs, ru-verbs with slightly different conjugation patterns and a couple of irregular verbs. Two kinds of adjectives and nouns also conjugate just like verbs. I-adjectives have their own conjugation endings and na-adjectives and nouns take copula or equivalence with "be" at the end in English.

The tenses in Japanese include present and past tense, but no future tense. Future events are usually described in the present tense. Also, unlike most other languages, Japanese has informal and super-polite endings of verbs and adjectives besides regular "masu" endings and for verbs "desu," endings for adjectives and copula. Informal expressions are commonly used among family members or close friends at school or work. When you get to know people well enough, you may start using short forms as you converse with them. However, it is not easy to know an appropriate time to switch to short forms. That is, permission to use short forms when one is addressing others at school according to work and age and seniority matters. Senior partners may feel justified to address in the short form, while expecting younger partners to continue to address in "masu" and "desu" ending expressions, since license to use short form is not mutual[101]. Japanese call this super-polite expressions "敬語" (keigo) or "respectful language" and use them to address the elderly, superiors at work and customers.

There is no distinction between singular and plural in most Japanese nouns, similar to "sheep" or "fish" in English, so the

101 Eri Banno, Ono, Yutaka, et al. Genki: An Integrated Course in elementary Japanese I, Vol. 1. Ibid.

numbers of items must be discovered based on context. As stated previously, very often Japanese add "tachi" after nouns for people (hito-tachi) and some animals to indicate they are plural. However, for inanimate objects like apples and peaches, there is no way to tell if they are singular or plural. Perhaps, there is a philosophical assumption that number does not matter for inanimate objects. For instance, if you eat three peaches today, they are formless in your stomach and not plural any more. They often add "tachi" after cats (neko-tachi) and dogs (inu-tachi) since they are considered close to humans and recognized as companions. However, there is no way to add farm animals like chickens and cows. When they are slaughtered for meat, they transform into an unaccountable mass instead of separate entities.

Different speech styles in Japanese

As I stated in previous chapters, the Japanese language has a few different speech styles and people are expected to use an appropriate style depending on the circumstance. The custom to use different styles of expressions depending on the relationships with people, or their positions in the social hierarchy in Japan and other East Asia regions, most likely stemmed from Confucian ideology. Confucianism has a great emphasis on the importance of social hierarchies and respect for their elders and loyalty to their masters. This is nearly 2500 years old and very prevalent in the East Asia over two millennia. In most circumstances in public, Japanese address in "masu" and "desu" ending expressions, since they are standard and the most commonly used style.

[102]Dr. Eriko Sato, who wrote the first Dummy book on Japanese in 2002, contends that Japanese use different speech styles depending on whom they address. Sato affirms the previously mentioned formal or super-polite style of communication used when one addresses

102 Eriko Sato: Japanese for Dummies. (NJ, USA: Wiley Publishing, 2002)

his or her business customers, bosses, teachers and those who are much older than him or her. The correct style depends on both social hierarchy like positions and age, and social grouping such as insiders and outsiders. Sato also notes that the informal style can sound very friendly but somehow rude. On the other hand, the formal or super-polite style can sound very polite and courteous but cold and distant. Then, the expression with the "desu" and "masu" endings form a polite but neutral style which one can use when addressing classmates, colleagues, neighbors, friends' parents and all kinds of acquaintances. She maintains that it is safe to start conversations with any individuals from "masu-form" and gradually move towards super-polite and short-form styles. Sato contends that the informal expressions with short form endings are used to address close friends and family members like parents, children, and spouses. Teachers also use the short-form in addressing to their students, while they expect a response in "masu" form.

Introduction of Literacy to Japan

The literacy of Japanese developed rapidly after the 7th Century AD as the leadership vigorously imported Chinese knowledge and technologies in order to transform the nation into a more civilized and powerful one. The writing system is possibly the most well-known aspect of the language due to its complexity. In fact, a regular sample of written Japanese contains a liberal mixture of three separate systems.

One of them is the kanji (漢字) that has been described. Today there are about 2,000 kanji in regular use in Japan.

The other two systems, which are generically called kana, are much more simple because they are both syllabic; this perfectly suits the phonotactic structure of the spoken language. Like capital and lower case sets of letters in the Roman alphabets, the two kana systems cover the same phonetic territory but have different orthographic functions. Katakana, the first syllabary, is more angular and is used mostly for transcribing words of foreign origin, such as terebi (television). Hiragana is more cursive, and can be used for grammatical inflections or for writing native Japanese words where kanji are not used. Using the inflected verb 書きます (kakimasu) as an example, the root ka- would be represented by the kanji carrying its meaning (write), and the inflection -kimasu would be written with three hiragana. This complexity at least partly owed to the fact that Japanese adopted the writing system from China. The Chinese language ha a significantly different syntax from Japanese, Korean or any other Ural-Altaic language family in the 7th Century AD.

Leadership of Prince Shotoku

The Japanese had no writing system prior to the introduction of the Chinese characters, which was originally used by Chinese people who lived in Japan during the early Christian era. [103]However, after the 7th Century, a writing system was finally introduced to Japan by these Chinese immigrants. The first writing in the country came into existence during the *Nara Period* (710 - 794) that saw the first signs of a tangible culture. It was also significant that the first historical records were kept during this era. The city of Nara bloomed and prospered as the first metropolitan capital of Japan and was considerably larger than it is today.

Under [104]*Shotoku Taishi* (聖徳太子) Prince Shotoku (574-622), a regent, son of [105]Emperor Yōmei (d. 587) and nephew of [106]Empress Suiko (d. 628), the nation was transformed radically with significant

---

103 Yaeko Sato Habein. The history of the Japanese written language (Tokyo, Japan: University of Tokyo Press, 1984)

104 Wikipedia: Prince Shōtoku. Online at http://en.wikipedia.org/wiki/Prince_ Shotoku

105 Wikipedia: Emperor Yōmei. Online at http://en.wikipedia.org/wiki/Emperor_ Yomei_of_Japan

106 Wikipedia: Empress Suiko. Online at http://en.wikipedia.org/wiki/Empress_ Suiko

and dramatic developments in many different fields including establishment of a centralized imperial stae system and constitution. The culture of the Imperial court was heavily influenced by Chinese political philosophies that arrived via Korea and passed through the capital to the rest of the country. During the Nara Period, Japan acquired various skills from the continent such as weaving, metalworking, tanning and shipbuilding as well as medicine, astronomy and Chinese characters. Confucianism was also introduced at this time. At this time the educated Japanese people began to study Chinese to acquire new knowledge and information not available in their country and to write down what they studied, so that they could teach the next generation.

[107]The earliest known examples of Japanese writing, dating back to the 5th and 6th centuries AD, were proper names inscribed with Chinese characters on a mirror and a sword (鏡 and 剣). But by the 8th and 9th centuries AD, Chinese characters began to be used to represent the Japanese language. Since the two verbal languages are so different in their syntax and phonology, Chinese loan words and characters began to be "Japanified" for more convenient use.

---

107 Isao Komatsu. The Japanese people. Origins of the people and the language.
     (Tokyo, Japan: Kokusai Bunka Shinkokai -The Society for International
     Cultural Relations, 1962).

[108]Prince Shotoku (聖徳太子) & his sons[109].

---

108 Was available August 2012: http http://www.lcv.ne.jp/~kohnoshg/site43/71.jpg
109 The picture is used under "fair dealing" (Canada) and "fair use" (USA)
     provisions in copyright law.

[110] File:Cangjie.jpg - Wikipedia [111].

---

110 Was available September 2012: http://en.wikipedia.org/wiki/Cangjie

111 The picture is used under "fair dealing" (Canada) and "fair use" (USA) provisions in copyright law.

NOTES

8

FORMATION OF JAPANESE LANGUAGE EDUCATION & TEXTBOOKS

General Overview

Japanese language education has a relatively short history in comparison to many other academic disciplines. There was virtually no discussion on the topic of teaching the language to non-Japanese until the late 1960s, except for the period in which Imperial Japan colonized some East Asian nations and forced them to study the language during the Second World War. Teaching Japanese to foreigners became taboo during the first decade after the war. For those who lived outside of Japan, particularly in her neighboring countries, the language had a strong association with the war, imperialism, colonization, atrocity and abuses by the imperial soldiers.

However, the discipline of Japanese language education had a rapid and significant development after the 1970s following the skyrocketing of the country's economy. At this time, the Japanese nation obtained the recognition as an economic super power. After the mid-70s, numerous Japanese language schools and teacher's training programs mushroomed all over Japan and some regions outside the country. There was a time when these private institutions prospered and obtained a tremendous amount of "bubble money" since they grew more rapidly than academic programs in colleges and universities.

These academic programs at colleges and universities developed slower than the language schools inside and outside the country. During the era that colleges did not offer Japanese language, prospective students had to attend the private language schools. Japanese nationals who were inspired to become language teachers for non-Japanese had to enrol in private teacher's training programs, since colleges did not offer the pedagogical/androgogical courses of the language. Surprisingly, the academic programs for non-Japanese in the country grew more slowly than those outside perhaps because those who lived outside of Japan felt more pressing needs to study Japanese.

After the early 1990s, Japan slipped into a recession after the long, booming "bubble economy" ended. The number of students continued to drop and the discipline of Japanese language education stagnated. However, after 2010, the number of students started to grow again. [112]It was likely the outcome of the phenomena that I have named the "*anime* and *manga* diaspora" or the dispersion of new media from Japan. The rapid dispersion of *anime,* or Japanese animation and *manga* or Japanese comic books to the world after the 1990s and the development of the Otaku culture worldwide also became an impetus among the younger generation to study Japanese. This could be considered similar to how German became considered the professional language for medical professionals in the 19th and early 20th centuries. In the same way, it is safe to conclude that Japanese is becoming the language for anime and manga professionals in the 21st century.

Tatsuya Nagashima's Unique Andragogy of Language Education

In the brief history of this discipline, there are many well respected individuals who contributed to the development of this

---

112 Isao Ebihara. All The World Is Anime. (Dayton, TN: USA: Global Ed Advance Press, 2010)

study. One of the significant forerunners who contributed to the field of Japanese language education is Tatsuya Nagashima (1930 – 2006). He was one of the greatest pioneers who started an enterprise to teach Japanese as a foreign language to non-Japanese people in early 1980s, when the majority of academics inside and outside of Japan did not recognize it as an academic discipline. He was an individual who anticipated the advent of new era to "boldly go where no man has gone before".

Nagashima was born in Osaka in 1930 as the fourth child among six children with Roman Catholic parents. The family experienced financial difficulty after he lost his father at age six. When he was 13, during the midst of the Second World War, Nagashima was left with a Roman Catholic priest originally from Germany. He lived the next three years with the priest and received strict discipline both academically and in his personal life. The training he received from the priest greatly impacted his whole life as a language educator and a scholar of religious studies. He learned Latin, German, and English from the priest and prepared for college while attending high school.

Nagashima went to the Roman Catholic Sophia University in Tokyo and majored in philosophy and Catholic theology, while vigorously studying languages like French and Spanish along with Latin, English and German taught by the priest who mentored him in his pre-teen years. However, he did not receive training to be a professional linguist or language educator. Nevertheless, he was well versed in many languages when he worked as a Japanese language educator, because of his intense training in Latin, German, English, French and Spanish. Nagashima had also some limited knowledge of Koine Greek, since he was required to study it at Sophia University and Protestant Seinan Gakuin Theological Seminary in Fukuoka.

After completing a master's program in Sophia University, Nagashima joined the order of the Jesuits, or Society of Jesus, and prepared himself for ordination as a Roman Catholic priest. However, he left the order before the ordination took place because he began to raise serious questions about Catholicism. He married a woman whom he met in a Catholic church and then converted to Baptist, and became a pastor after graduating from Seinan Gakuin Theological Seminary. Later, Nagashima went to Andover Newton Theological School located in Newton, Massachusetts to complete his second master's degree.

During the time he was a Baptist pastor, he opened several foreign language institutes to teach English, German, French and Latin to Japanese nationals. However, he was not satisfied with the enterprise simply to teach foreign languages to Japanese nationals. Nagashima seriously contemplated starting a completely new kind of institution to teach foreigners the Japanese language. He foresaw the era when non-Japanese began to learn Japanese. He could well have been influenced by the number of American business people who worshiped at Tokyo Baptist Church where he pastored and closely observed what they wanted. Perhaps, some of them told him of their pressing need to learn Japanese to operate their businesses successfully over there. In 1976, Nagashima opened PanaLinga Institute in Tokyo to teach Japanese to foreigners and simultaneously train Japanese nationals as language teachers. He also resigned from the pastorate and left the Baptist denomination since he started asking serious questions about Protestant doctrine.

After leaving the Baptist denomination Nagashima and his wife briefly returned to the Catholic Church and contemplated their spiritual direction. After a long contemplation and research, he finally came to the conclusion that the [113]General Church of the New Jerusalem which follows the teaching of Emanuel Swedenborg (1688 – 1772) is most agreeable to his theology. He and his wife flew to Bryn Athyn,

---

113 Wikipedia: General Church of the New Jerusalem. Online at http://en.wikipedia.org/wiki/General_Church_of_the_New_Jerusalem

Pennsylvania and visited the headquarters of the denomination to join the organization as the first members from Japan. After joining the General Church, Nagashima spent his remaining life and energy to translate Swedenborg's work into Japanese, while still training Japanese nationals as language instructors. However, he never pursued ordination as a clergy of the organization, being completely content with the status of laity.

In 1992, Nagashima resigned from PanaLinga Institute and moved to Tokushima to teach the Japanese language. He taught Japanese language teaching methodology, English and religious studies as a professor at Shikoku University. Toru Sakamoto, who studied the Japanese language teaching method under Nagashima took over the directorship of PanaLinga Institute. In the early 2000s, Nagashima retired from Shikoku University, but continued to live in Tokushima until his death in 2006. He spent his last six years exclusively in translating Swedenborg's Latin text into Japanese.

After the time of opening PanaLinga Institute in Tokyo, Nagashima became a prolific author and completed numerous publication projects including a couple of textbooks. Unlike most other Japanese language textbooks in the 1980s, his works contain socio-linguistic and anthropological insights. He could be considered the forerunner of "communicative method" in Japanese language androgogy since his textbooks are dialogical and socio-linguistically based. Because Nagashima acquired a wider variety of education in humanity than typical language educators of his day who had studied only linguistics or philology at universities, he impressed many students with his encyclopedic knowledge and unique perspectives and insights. Nagashima possessed intercultural and interdisciplinary insights as well as socio-linguistic and other insights and shared them in his class and publications. Various statements in his books and newsletters were also social prophetic and contain the timeless truth foreseeing the era of globalization regarding the planet becoming one community, before the terms "globalism" or "globalization" came into existence.

It is safe to conclude that language education was not his sole interest. The other academic fields that interested him throughout his life included religion, theology and philosophy.

[114]After starting PanaLinga Institute in Tokyo, in addition to writing textbooks of the Japanese language in 1980 and 1982, he wrote several others publications on Japanese language education and cross-cultural studies for Japanese nationals in the 1980s and 1990s. In these years, Nagashima developed his own unique andragogy while teaching Japanese to adult foreign students and language teaching methodology to mostly Japanese young adults.

In the 1980s, Japanese language education was in the dawning era and the world started recognizing the need to develop the field as a new academic discipline. Numerous new training institutions for language teachers came into existence in that era and were in competition with one another. Most of these institutions taught the "direct method" or teaching Japanese language using only Japanese, even to beginners. Nagashima was strongly against the trend to use the direct method exclusively and remarked that it was terribly inefficient and time consuming. He believed that its exclusive use only boosts puffed up egos of lazy and narcissistic teachers and confused and frustrated students.

Instead, he taught his trainees that students benefit the most when teachers teach Japanese grammar and background cultural factors in plain English, Chinese, Korean or any other mother tongue of the students. Nagashima had a philosophical assumption that teachers must acquire at least one foreign language before teaching any language to them. He or she also must work hard to study

114 Tatsuya Nagashima, Japanese in 30 Weeks I: Romanji Course. (Tokyo, Japan: PanaLinga Institute, 1980)

students' mother tongues although the acquisition to a level of fluency is impossible. Nagashima's philosophy of language instruction seems to be inherited from the Roman Catholic priest who mentored him. At the same time, he believed that the class must be interactive and provide students enough time to practice Japanese expressions in front of the teacher and peers instead of spending most of class time merely listening to teachers' lectures on grammar.

Nagashima also viewed it unpractical and wasteful that some academics during 1980s tried to apply [115]Noam Chomsky's (b. 1928 -) [116]generative grammar to Japanese language education. The generative grammar is highly theoretical and mathematically oriented and very difficult to comprehend for the average educational practitioner without a science background. Nagashima regarded the generative grammar as an intellectual game and grammar consisted of grammar for grammar's sake or theory for theory's sake, so he did not give any credit to it.

Because Nagashima majored in philosophy in his undergrad and first master's degree, he had an excellent opportunity to develop his own educational theory and andragogy. His educational philosophy was consistently Socratic and student centered. Therefore, he greatly respected students' inherent characters, qualities, attributes, and potentials to grow and become himself or herself. He firmly believed that the educator's role is to bring out and activate what the Creator has already given the students instead of simply installing something completely new to their minds.

Nagashima developed a new grammatical system of Japanese language based on Latin grammar. Prior to the era in which he developed a new grammar, it is safe to conclude that there was

115 Wikipedia: Noam Chomsky. Online at http://en.wikipedia.org/wiki/Noam_Chomsky

116 Wikipedia: Generative Grammar. Online at http://en.wikipedia.org/wiki/Generative_grammar

no adequate grammar for non-Japanese learners of the language. Although there were several areas which required improvement, Nagashima's grammar was innovative and an extremely significant contribution to the world of the Japanese language education. Before his work, "kokubunpo", (国文法) or "national grammar", was the only grammatical system for the Japanese language. It was designed only for teaching Japanese children instead of non-Japanese adult students, and notoriously confusing and inefficient for both foreign students and Japanese nationals. Also, most Japanese language schools and teacher training institutions that advocated the exclusive use of the direct method had adopted "kokubunpo" as a teaching method in the 1980s.

The greatest accomplishment of Nagashima as a Japanese language educator is the systematization of Japanese verb conjugation and the creation of a plain enough conjugation table for learners. As mentioned previously, Japanese has u-verbs, ru-verbs and a couple of irregular verbs with various different conjugational endings including present and past tense. Dealing with ru-verbs is not so problematic for learners because they all conjugate in the same pattern. However, u-verbs have many different breeds or subspecies with different conjugation patterns and greatly confuse learners at the beginners' level. His textbook identifies u-verbs as Group One Verbs and ru-verbs Group Two Verbs.

Likely Nagashima was the first person who tried to explain the maze of u-verb conjugations in a systematized table and plain enough English, although the information in his textbook was still on the lengthy side and overwhelmingly massive to many students. [117]In his textbook, Nagashima included 19 model verbs for four conjugation patterns (infinitive, masu-form, negative root, and participle). These verbs are 17 u-verbs just as kau (to buy), iu (to say), yatou (to hire),

---

117 Tatsuya Nagashima, Japanese in 30 Weeks I: Romanji Course. Ibid.

suwaru (to sit), hairu (to enter), uru (to sell), kaeru (to go back), noru (to get on/in), matsu (to wait), iku (to go), kaku (to write), hanasu (to speak), yobu (to call), nomu (to drink), isogu (to hurry), a couple of ru-verbs just as miru (to see), taberu (to eat) and kuru (to come) and suru (to do), a couple of only irregular verbs that Japanese has. The infinitive is called "dictionary form" in newer textbooks, since it is the form that is found in the dictionary. The five columns of the table include English translation, infinitive (dictionary form), masu-form negative root and participle (te-form) and looks like the following:

English	Infinitive	Masu-form	Negative root	Participle
to buy	ka-u	ka-i-masu	ka-wa-nai	ka-t-te
to say	i-u	i-i-masu	i-wa-nai	i-t-te
to hire	yato-u	yato-i-masu	yato-wa-nai	yato-t-te
to sit	Suwar-u	suwar-i-masu	suwar-a-nai	suwa-t-te
to enter	Hair-u	hair-i-masu	hair-a-nai	hai-t-te
to sell	ur-u	ur-i-masu	ur-a-nai	u-t-te
to to go back	kaer-u	kaer-i-masu	kaer-a-nai	kae-t-te
to get on/in	nor-u	nor-i-masu	nor-a-nai	no-t-te
to wait	mats-u	mach-i-masu	mat-a-nai	ma-t-te
to go	ik-u	ik-i-masu	ik-a-nai	i-t-te
to write	kak-u	kak-i-masu	kak-a-nai	ka-i-te
to speak	hanas-u	hanash-i-masu	hana-sa-nai	hanash-i-te
to call	yob-u	yob-i-masu	yob-a-nai	yo-n-de
to drink	nom-u	nom-i-masu	nom-a-nai	no-n-de
to hurry	isog-u	isog-i-masu	isog-a-nai	iso-i-de
to see	mi-ru	m-i-masu	m-i-nai	m-i-te
to eat	tabe-ru	tab-e-masu	tab-e-nai	tab-e-te
to come	ku-ru	k-i-masu	k-o-nai	k-i-te
to do	su-ru	sh-i-masu	sh-i-nai	sh-i-te

Fifteen verbs in the first and largest row of the table are u-verbs with a variety of conjugational endings particularly in the te-form. The second row contains a couple of ru-verbs and the third row a couple of irregular verbs. These two are only irregular verbs and somehow similar to ru-verbs in terms of conjugational endings. As the table indicates, Nagashima treats Japanese verbs as life-forms with two segments when they are in the "infinitive" or the dictionary form and creatures with three divisions like insects, when they are in other forms. These body parts are stem, infix or the middle part and the inflection or the very end. Only the dictionary form does not have the infix in the Nagashima textbook. In order to explain three components of a verb, Nagashima created the following table[118] :

	Group One Verb	Group Two Verbs
Infinitive	ka-u	m-i-ru
Masu-form	ka-i-masu	m-i-masu
Negative root	ka-wa-nai	m-i-nai
Participle	ka-tte	m-i-te

Nagashima maintains that all verbs have three components; a stem or unchangeable part, inflectional endings at the end, and "infix" or middle part to intervene two portions euphonically to make the verb sounds smooth.

Nagashima called most basic dictionary forms "infinitive" probably because of his study of Latin and many other European languages. It is the form that is found in the dictionary and textbook index. The "masu-form" is most commonly used in Japanese daily conversations and almost all textbooks at the beginner level start from the masu-form. It does not include extremely polite expressions but formal enough that people may use to address almost any individuals

---

118 Tatsuya Nagashima, Grammatica Japonica. (Tokyo, Japan: PanaLinga Institute, 1996)

including superiors and elders. The "negative root" is the root form through which numerous negative expressions are formulated by adding various endings.

The "participle" in Nagashima's definition is called "te-form" in most textbooks today. The te-form conjugation of u-verbs are one of the most confusing and frustrating areas in Japanese language study for most beginners. Likely he used this terminology because it has a function to describe a continuing action just like the participle in many other languages such as English, German, Latin and Greek by adding the ending "imasu". However, the te-form is more versatile and multi-functional than a "participle" in Indo-European languages. It is used to ask, give or deny permission, forming a sentence that describes more than two actions or events by adding various endings. By adding "mo iidesu", one can give others permission or deny permission by adding "wa ikemasen". An example of giving permission is "Anata wa Ocha o nonde mo iidesu" (You may drink tea) and an example of denying permission is "Anata wa tabako o suttee wa ikemasen" (You are not allowed to smoke a cigarette). One can combine more than two actions by inserting the te-form prior to a main action like "Udon o tabe-te sake o nomimasu" (I eat udon and drink sake).

Nagashima's Contribution

Although Nagashima's androgogy and grammar was established in the 1980s is somewhat outdated, his philosophy of education is still relevant, ageless and even prophetic. In the introduction of his textbook, Nagashima contended "the Japanese language is the indispensable key, with which Japanese art, thought, and science, long locked up in the islands of Japan, can be opened for the use of all human society". He maintained that the Japanese culture as a whole must be utilized to enrich the entire human population on this planet. Then, the language is the key to decode this enigmatic and cryptic cultural content. In his Japanese teacher training course at PanaLinga Institute, he introduced Cang Jie as the inventor of Chinese charactors. He was portrayed as possessing two pairs of eyes and eight pupils, since he was an extraordinarily ingenious man who could foresee the future. In many senses, Nagashima, like Cang Jie, anticipated the remote future way beyond his time and left an indispensable intellectual inheritance to those of the next generation.

Nagashima's systematization of Japanese grammar and attempt to explain verb conjugation has passed on to newer textbooks and is still being published today.

Japanese Language Education for the Third Millenium

Current textbook writers now compete with each other to create the most user-friendly and student centered works. Japanese language textbooks have made rapid progress from the age of the dysfunuctional "kokubunpo". For instance, [119]the Genki textbook published by Japan Times and widely used in colleges and universities in North America has similar explanations as Nagashima in dealing with verbs. However, Genki authors simplify the grammar further with regard to all verbs as a species with only two body parts in all circumstances. They also use different terminologies than Nagashima and have renamed the portion called "stem" by most grammarians into the "verb base" and the "inflection" into "suffix". For instance, the stem of the verb "taberu" or to eat is "tabe" and "ru" is the suffix. In masu-form, the inflection "ru" is simply replaced with "masu". Likewise, all other ru-verbs have the same conjugation patterns that the portion prior to "masu" in the dictionary form never changes. However, they treat the infix as a part of the suffix instead of a separate component. For instance, when the verb "iku" or to go formulates the masu-form, the suffix "u" is replaced by "imasu".

---

119 Eri Banno, Ono, Yutaka, et al. Genki: An Integrated Course in elementary
      Japanese I, Vol. 1, (Tokyo, Japan: Japan Times Press, 1999/2002)

Nagashima viewed the ru-verb as having two classes and included "miru" (to see) as an example with "i" and "taberu" (to eat) as another example with "e" respectively prior to the final "ru". However, Genki authors treat all ru-verbs as one species since they all conjugate in the same way. All ru-verbs have the same endings for the dictionary form, masu-form, negative root and te-form. Also, no matter whether they are one part or two parts and called "stem" or "base", the entire section before the inflection is unchangeable. For "miru", "mi" is an unchangeable part as well as "tabe" of "taberu".

This explanation seems user friendlier than Nagashima's conjugational table when dealing with the ru-verb, since "tabe" is a solid and unchangeable part when the verb takes all conjugational patterns. However, I have some objection to Genki's explanation to treat the middle "i" as a part of the ending of u-verbs. Although I understand that it was a serious attempt to simplify the verb conjugation, a too long ending seems to confuse many learners. It sounds a little unnatural and unnecessarily stretches the ending starting with "i" or "e".

Therefore, I usually teach ru-verb as verbs with only two segments exactly as the Genki textbook teaches. However, I follow the explanation of Nagashima's textbook in explaining the u-verbs as a creature with three body parts except when they are in dictionary form. For beginners, it seems easier to comprehend that the middle part is "i" when it is the masu-form and "a" in the negative than the explanation that the ending has a drastic transformation.

As mentioned in the previous chapter, there is also a pitfall for many beginners to assume all verbs with ru-endings in the dictionary form are ru-verbs. Just like all ru-verbs, many of them have "ru" endings in the dictionary form and many learners find it overwhelmingly difficult to differentiate between the two. If the vowels "a", "u", or "o" are observed right before the final "ru", they are certainly u-verbs as mentioned in Chapter Two. If the vowels "i" or "e" appear prior to the final "ru", they are usually ru-verbs with some exceptions like "neru" (to sleep) and "kaeru" (to go back).

In contrast to Nagashima, Genki's authors explain the grammar of te-form with "hiragana" and some kanji instead of Romanization because they expect students to know Japanese writing systems by the time they complete the second lesson. The te-form appears in Lesson 6, and students are supposed to master all hiragana and some kanji long before studying te-form. Genki created six categories of u-verbs. First ones are those which end in "u" (う), "tsu" (つ) and "ru" (る). The examples are "au: 会う" (to meet), "matsu: 待つ" (to wait) or, and "toru: とる" (to take). They all have the ending with ":つ て tte" or the ending with double consonants and "te". Te-form ending of "au: 会う" is "atte: 会って", "matsu: 待つ" is "matte: 待って", and "toru: とる" is "totte: とって".

The second category is the u-verbs ending with final "mu" (む), "bu" (ぶ) and "nu" (ぬ). Examples are "yomu: 読む" (to read), "asobu: 遊ぶ" (to plaay) and "shinu: 死ぬ" (to die). They have the "nde:んで" ending in the te-form. In the te-form, "yomu: 読む" is "yonde: 読んで", "asobu: 遊ぶ" is "asonde: 遊んで" and "shinu: 死ぬ" is "shinde: 死んで".

The third category is the u-verbs ending with final "ku" (く), and the example is "kaku: 書く" (to write). The te-form of "kaku: 書く" is "kaite: 書いて". Only exception among "ku" ending verbs is "iku: 行く" (to go), and its' te-form is "itte: 行って". The fourth category is the u-verbs ending with final "gu" (ぐ), and the example is "oyogu: 泳ぐ" (to swim). The te-form of "oyogu: 泳ぐ" is "oyoide: 泳いで". The fifth category is the u-verbs ending with final "su" (す), and the example is "hanasu: 話す" (to speak). The te-form of "hanasu: 話す" is "hanashite: 話して".

For some beginners, grammatical explanations with hiragana are threatening, and this is why Nagashima wrote the beginners book with Romanization only. However, for those who already know Japanese writings, hiragana is symbolic and somehow helpful to memorize patterns. For instance, small "tsu" (っ) is the character to indicate only double consonants, and students may easily associate "u" (う) "tsu" (つ) ru" (る) in the dictionary form with the small "tsu" (っ) and "te" endings in the te-form.

In Genki text, there is also an exercise to memorize the te-form of various kinds of u-verbs by singing the "Te-form Song" with the melody of the Battle Hymn of the Republic. The first verse of the Te-form Song reads: "au (to meet) atte, matsu (to wait) matte, toru (to take) totte yomu (to read) yonde, asobu (to play) asonde, shinu (to die) shinde kaku (to write) kaite, kesu (to erase) keshite, isogu (to hurry) isoide mina u verb te form. Then, the second verse is: "u tsu ru - te mu bu nu - nde ku - ite gu - ide su - shite u-verb te form".

The Te-form Song reinforces students' understanding of various u-verb endings, so that they can memorize by repeating and chanting. The last part, "u tsu ru - te mu bu nu - nde ku - ite gu - ide" (うつる ってむぶぬんでくいてぐいで) "su - shite" (すして) u-verb te form" indicates the relationship between the dictionary form ending and te-form ending and implant the patterns to the unconscious realm of the students' minds through constant repetition.

TheTe-form Song is becoming a very popular item and various textbook writers, educators, and even some students have created their own versions. If the student finds the Battle Hymn of the Republic too dated, he or she can use any contemporary music such as Rock, Pop, Country or the melody of anime movies. Some ambitious learners of Japanese have uploaded their own versions of Te-form Songs to YouTube and other popular sites on the internet.

For the majority of learners, the acquisition of verb conjugation, particularly te-form, is tedious and time consuming. The process of learning any language requires a great deal of repetition. The Te-form Song could be considered a great invention since it reduces the pain of language learning significantly.

Japanese Language for the Otaku Generation

Otakue generation language learners, who started learning after the *anime* and *manga* diaspora, are quite different from traditional language learners in many different ways. Their learning motives stem from the anime and manga world. They also like to learn the Te-form Song because it is a popular and efficient tool. But Otaku learners often create very innovative video presentations and upload them to YouTube. Many different versions of the song on YouTube created by Otaku Japanese learners come with various different melodies. Some of these, including one from the Vocaloid Miku Hatsune, was discussed in a previous chapter.

The main motive for these learners is the acquisition of easier access to the anime and manga world. They prefer reading manga to textbooks or any other ordinary materials like novels, magazines or newspapers. They use anime movies for the acquisition of auditory or listening skills. Many of them are also inspired to become professionals who produce anime and manga. In other words, these individuals study Japanese as a professional language through which they understand the media and make their living.

Some of these individuals also tend to study the language alone without being enrolled in Japanese classes in college and universities or language schools. Otaku individuals are often extremely independent, individualistic and do not utilize traditional social places like colleges and sports clubs to find friends and potential mates. The only place in which they socialize and meet friends is the internet. Therefore, they study the language almost exclusively from the media like anime, manga, YouTube video and other materials from the internet. In some extreme cases, they often end up speaking Japanese like anime and manga characters. There is a problem if they are able to speak only in this way failing to acquire all other ways of the speech. There is an entertaining story that more than three decades ago a Japanese scholar who studied Shakespeare extensively, travelled to England and spoke Elizabethan English to people in London. People there were very perplexed and sent this gentleman to a mental institution because they came to the conclusion that he was insane. The same thing might happen to those who studied Japanese exclusively from anime and manga and travel to Japan and converse with people outside of the internet.

For instance, the first person pronoun or equivalency of "I" is gender specific in Japanese. "Watashi" (私) is a gender neutral expression that both male and female persons can use. However, "boku" (僕) and "ore" (俺), two commonly used first person pronouns are exclusively for males in standard Japanese. However, many female manga characters frequently use "boku" and "ore" as the first person pronoun referring to themselves. As a result, many female learners who are exclusively self-taught in Japanese, have no hesitation to refer to themselves as "boku" or "ore". It may sound cute in some contexts and many Otaku generation young adults in Japan do it. However, it is acceptable only in onversations with close friends, but not in social settings like a job (outside of anime/manga industries), job interviews, and interaction with customers.

Also, some popular anime and manga like [120]Naruto use esoteric expressions extensively. Naruto is a very popular graphic novel and anime movie in which a teenage Ninja recruit lives in a community named Hidden Leaf Village or Konohagakure no Sato (木ノ葉隠れの里). This is a product of Japanese modern day pop culture that

---

120 Wikepedia: Naruto. Online at http://en.wikipedia.org/wiki/Naruto

demonstrates the motif of the preternatural world and occultism and psychic power. Although the story setting is contemporary, characters in it use many dialects and archaic expressions, since they live in an imaginary Ninja world in the 21st century. These expressions are not in most dictionaries and the average Japanese person is not familiar with them. You can imagine how strange it is if any person in the real world in the 21st century uses the same expressions as Ninja do from the 16th century.

Although it is questionable to teach anime and manga products with many non-standard Japanese expressions to beginners, introducing them to intermediate and advanced level learners is completely acceptable and can benefit their learning. There is a pressing need to drastically modify and reconstruct the style of Japanese language learning in higher education. By doing this, we must accommodate the education to the younger generation with updated learning styles.

[121]Tatsuya Nagashima (left) at Christmas Party, 1984
(PanaLinga Institute).

---

121 The picture is taken by the author, 1984.

NOTES

Part 3

CULTURE NOTES

NOTES

9

FOOD, CITIES AND CELEBRATIONS

Numerous parts of Japan's culture are key to understanding it and its language. As food is an extremely important part of Japanese culture, I've taken the opportunity to give my own "tour" of the best foods and food spots in Japan as I've experienced them. In addition, I've highlighted some cities and their landmarks and Japanese celebrations, along with what is termed "urban legends" and YouTube and the culture. These are all simply an "opener" to a background understanding of Japan and the development of its language.

For Foodies

Tsukiji in Tokyo has the largest food market in the world and some of its restaurants are outstanding. You might experience a "foretaste of heaven" if you eat sushi, eel, suppon (soft-shell turtle) or any other fish. Nagano, however, is a mountainous region with limited access to fresh sea foods. However, it is considered the best place for wild edibles like fiddlehead, miso, soba noodle, peaches and apples. Dishes from game meat from deer and boars as well as beef, chicken and pork have also obtained excellent reputations. Although it is difficult to obtain fresh fish from the sea, the fresh water fish dishes are very good. If you are desperate for fish in Nagano, I recommend Ayu or Wakasagi's tempura. Both of these are small fish a little larger than goldfish, and chefs in local restaurants fry them as soon as you arrive.

[122]Soba (蕎麦) is a Japanese buckwheat noodle made from buckwheat flour and commonly consumed all over the country. It takes approximately three months for buckwheat to be ready for harvest, so the product can be harvested three times a year, in spring, summer, and autumn. Soba noodles are served either with a cold dipping sauce with wasabi and shredded green onions, or in a hot broth as a noodle soup with chili pepper and shredded green onions. Many established restaurants will serve both soba and udon as they are often served in a similar manner using the same soup and toppings. The buckwheat was originally considered a luxury item that only a limited number of aristocrats could afford to consume. However, the custom of eating buckwheat noodles among commoners in Edo or today's Tokyo started during the Edo Period (1603 - 1868), when the general population of Edo became considerably wealthy. Commoners in the city started eating soba while the rural population were still poor and not able to obtain the noodles and other gourmet items.

Izakaya is an inexpensive restaurant and pub which serves reasonably good food and drink at a lower price. If you live in Japan, you will find that Izakaya is a most friendly place for your wallet, though the food there is not the first class.

Shimokitazawa is located within a large district of Tokyo. It has rather an old fashioned appearance if you view it only from the outside, because most buildings are small and at least 30 years older. High-rise buildings are prohibited and streets around the train station are very narrow so that no vehicles can go through. However, merchandise in stores and food in restaurants are very fashionable and trendy, so that the town is always filled with young adults.

Tonkatsu, a breaded, deep-fried pork cutlet, generally served with shredded cabbage and/or miso soup, is a Japanese delicacy with Western influence that was introduced less than 200 years

---

122 Soba (蕎麦). Online at http://en.wikipedia.org/wiki/Soba

ago. Tonkatsu was originally introduced to Japan by the Portuguese, considered a type of yōshoku, that is, Japanese versions of European cuisine invented in the late 19th and early 20th centuries. The original Tonkatsu introduced from the west had a very rich flavor since it was fried in lard. However, they have invented a lighter version that is fried in sesame seed oil and canola oil because of health concerns. Tonkatsu today is most commonly eaten with a type of thick Japanese Worcestershire sauce called tonkatsu sauce that uses apple juice as a principal ingredient.

Kanda River is infamously dirty and smelly. However, it was once a very beautiful and clean river, as recent as 60 years ago, and used as an aqueduct of downtown Tokyo. After the 1960s, Japan's heavy industry grew rapidly and the economy boomed, but at the expense of a clean living environment for both people and other living creatures. Almost all fish and other fresh water creatures in big cities were dead or found refuge in rivers and lakes in the countrysides.

However, after the 1990s, clean living environments and ecosystem came to the forefront of the mind of the population and government. More strict regulations and bylaws for draining the industrious waste to rivers and lakes was put into place. Sumida River, much larger than Kanda River, was once filfthy like a huge sewage river. However, many people volunteered to clean the river and worked hard for more than a decade. Now, the river is gradually gaining its life back and has become attractive enough for tourists. Fish and other creatures have come back to the river. Likewise, Kanda River has improved over the last 20 years, but there is still room for improvement.

[123]Just like Chinese and several other people groups in East Asia, Japan has over 2000 years of history of proudly consuming すっぽん (suppon) or soft-shell turtles. Several districts of the country have

---

123 Wikipedia: Suppon. (スッポン). Online at http://ja.wikipedia.org/wiki/%E3%8
  2%B9%E3%83%83%E3%83%9D%E3%83%B3

different and distinct ways of preparing the suppon dish. Kyoto has several old and excellent suppon restaurants because this culinary custom originated in Kyoto. Traditionally in Kyoto, they serve a simple suppon hotpot with only turtle meat and its internal organs, green onions or chives, ginger root juice, mirin (Japanese sweet cooking wine) and a light colored soy sauce. In Tokyo and numerous other districts, suppon nabe (hotpot) is served with various kinds of vegetables. Because Kyoto's suppon hotpot does not include vegetables except green onions, the quality of meat is a vital factor. I recommend suppon in Daiichi Restaurant if you have a chance to visit Kyoto.

[124]Daiichi Restaurant in Kyoto, with over 300 years of history, strictly follows the local tradition to serve very plain suppon-nabe with no vegetables except green onions. The restaurant originally served suppon as a medicine to travelers, before modern Western medical science was introduced to the nation. The suppon meal in Daiichi maintains premier quality and exquisite taste, but costs over 20,000 yen per person and could be considered a little pricey for the average North American. However, there are many good suppon restaurants in most major cities in the nation which serve hotpot, sashimi and fried suppon of good enough quality for the average travelers with more reasonable prices than Daiichi.

If you are an advanced foodie, alternatively you could purchase live suppon in the Tsukiji Food Market in Tokyo, combat the creature on your own and create your own suppon nabe. However, you will have to spend money for a deba butcher knife first which is quite expensive, but a good investment if you love cooking. The knife works very well when you cut large fish, crabs and lobsters besides suppon. Surprisingly, soft-shell turtles are four-legged creatures which contain Omega 3 fatty acids instead of Omega 6. It indicates that suppon fat

---

124 すっぽん料理大市. Online at http://www.suppon-daiichi.com/about/

and cholesterol are nearly identical with vegetables. If you are a veggie hater but want to stay healthy, the consumption of this wonderful creature might be a way for you to stay healthy.

Eating blowfish at home can in fact be a bit dangerous. It is not legal to cook fugu or blowfish on your own and in your own house unless you have a professional license to prepare it. This is because the fish contains a poison called Tetrodotoxin in their organs. If you want to try fugu, go to a restaurants with a qualified chef who can remove their organs safely. It is generally on the expensive side, but you will enjoy it if you are fish lover.

During the Edo period (1603 - 1868), Japanese people were discouraged from eating meat because of the Buddhist teaching that pursued vegetarianism. Though Buddhism was not able to eliminate meat consumption completely, their teaching had a significant impact from the medieval to the early modern era. People ate chickens, wild avian, and rabbit meat, but never consumed pork and beef because large mammals were considered reincarnated humans. They ate rabbits because they were considered kin to avian because of their size, although they are fully mammals. Surprisingly, some Japanese consumed canine meat for medicinal reasons.

The Dojo Loach, a freshwater fish consumed widely among the Japanese gourmet population is commonly referred to as a Weather Loach or Weatherfish, because of their their habit of becoming very active when there is a change in the weather. Unfortunately, dojo lauch as a delicacy is hardly known in the general North American public. The fish are only about 12 cm in length and prefer deep muddy pools where the water flows slowly. The fish slightly resemble eels that come from both wild and fish farms. The Japanese have consumed dojo since antiquity or the prehistoric era. The Dojo Loach was the most commonly eaten fish among the working class around the 17th to 19th centuries. During the Edo Period the restaurant industry blossomed in major Japanese cities, and the Dojo Loach was served there regularly.

The oldest Dojo restaurant in existence now is [125]駒形どぜう (Komagata Dojo)[126] in Tokyo's Asakusa district. The restaurant was founded in 1801 and has developed a number of significant dojo recipes during the past few centuries. It is located in a traditional Japanese style building and equipped with old-fashioned furnishings, zabuton cushions, tatami mats and low tables. The fish is cooked on a small *hibachi* grill brought to the table, with the charcoal already red-hot, immediately after ordering the meal. The menu features exotic dishes like *dojo* miso-soup, どじょうなべ (dojo-nabe) or a miso-based hotpot dish with thinly sliced gobo (burdock) root and *dojo* that have been slit and spread open 柳川なべ (Yanagawa-nabe) with beaten egg poured over the same ingredient as *dojo-nabe* except the sauce is soy-sauce based instead of miso[127].

Komagata Dojo has two versions of dojo-nabe. The first one is the traditional dojo-nabe in which live dojo fish are grilled with gobo, sake and miso in a shallow pan with a lid. After the fish are cooked, the lid is removed, green onions added and it is simmered for a few minutes. The whole fish including the head is eaten. The fish is very tender and tasty. The second version is called どじょうさきなべ (dojo saki nabe) in which the heads are removed and the fish is gutted and deboned before going to the pot. This is more user friendly to dojo newbies and foreign tourists since they don't have to eat the head and other parts. Likewise, Komagata Dojo's Yanagawa-nabe includes prepared fish such as dojo saki nabe. I strongly encourage you to dine in this over 300 year-old restaurant in Tokyo when you visit the city.

125 Komagata Dojo (駒形どぜう). Online at http://www.dozeu.com
126 In Komagata Dojo, they transcribe Hiragana どぜう instead of どじょう. The restaurant proudly retains the old fashioned transcription in Edo Period, in which they inargurated the business.
127 NIPPONIA No. 41 June 15, 2007: Bon Appetit! Japanese Culture in the Kitchen. Online at http://web-japan.org/nipponia/nipponia41/en/appetit/appetit01.html

[128] 駒形どぜう (Komagata Dojo) [129].

Shamo (軍鶏 or シャモ) is a breed of gourmet chicken which was originated in Thailand that was imported to Japan during the early Edo period. This breed is extremely aggressive since it was originally used as fighting cocks when cockfighting was still legal. After the game was banned in Japan, they highly valued the breed because of the exceptionally good taste. The meat is a little tougher than average chickens and has a stronger taste and flavor. Many districts of the country have their own breed of Shamo with distinct taste. Among them, Tokyo Shamo is most well known and accessible for tourists. Shamo Nabe (hotpot), Yakitori or Oyakodon in one of the finest Shamo

---

[128] Was available September 2012http://minkara.carview.co.jp/userid/282450/spot/485222/

[129] The picture is used under "fair dealing" (Canada) and "fair use" (USA) provisions in copyright law.

restaurants is a "must" experience when you tour the Japanese capital[130].

[131]The お好み焼き (Okonomiyaki) is a Japanese savoury pancake containing a variety of ingredients like prawns, pork, beef, chicken and various types of vegetables. The batter is made of flour, grated nagaimo or a kind of taro, water with dashi (bonito and kelp extract), eggs and shredded cabbage, and usually contains other ingredients such as green onion, meat (generally pork or bacon), octopus, squid, shrimp, vegetables, kimchi, mochi or cheese. After pouring the batter, the chef quickly add main ingredients, adds more batter on top, flips it over and grills it for a few minutes before serving. In the Hiroshima area, the main ingredient is noodles and the quantity is more generous than any other district in Japan. Some okonomiyaki restaurants use grill-it-yourself style, where the server produces a bowl of raw ingredients and customers mix and grill their own dish at tables fitted with special hotplates.

In the feast of New Year's celebration, each region of the country serves distinct Osechi and Zoni soup and takes great pride in their recipes. People in coastal regions almost always enjoy seafood based Osechi and Zoni soup for the entire month of January. People in some mountain regions, however, enjoy Osechi and Zoni based on land products, since they have developed a culinary taste for meat of avian, farm and wild animals and varieties of vegetables.

Those in various mountainous regions remote from the coast customarily consume shark meat as an Osechi meal item during the New Year celebrations, since it was the only seafood that was available in these districts during the pre-modern era. Since sharks do not posess bladders, they contain ammonia in their meat and so can last much longer than other seafoods without refrigeration.

---

130 Wikipedia: Shamo (chicken). Online at http://en.wikipedia.org/wiki/Shamo_ (chicken)

131 Wikipedia: Okonomiyaki. Online at http://en.wikipedia.org/wiki/Okonomiyaki

Shark meat with ammonia flavor was considered a rare delicacy more than a century ago, although the avarage Japanese today finds it distasteful. Apart from Osechi meal in mountain regions, some Tokyoites enjoy Shark Nikogori or Jelly of the soup of cooked fish. They simmer shark's meat and skin with soy sauce, mirin and kelp dashi for 30 to 40 minutes and then refrigerate about two hours. Because shark itself is very gelatinous, there is no need to add gelatin. Shark Nikogori is served in many Izakaya restaurants around Tokyo since it is considered best to eat Nikogori with either shochu or sake.

Most Westerners in Japan are reluctant at first to eat any kind of reptiles. However, they often taste a small bit of suppon after being persistently persuaded to eat it by a Japanese national. Then, many of them find it very tasty and decide to eat more. Strangely enough, some of them become hooked on the rare delicacy and visit a suppon restaurant repeatedly.

[132]Ramen (ラーメン) is a Japanese noodle dish with Chinese-style wheat noodles served in a pork bone, chicken bone or fish-based broth, often flavored with soy sauce or miso, and using toppings such as sliced pork called chāshū, dried seaweed called nori, kamaboko or fish cake, green onions, and occasionally corn. Almost every local community in Japan has its own distinct variety of ramen, from the tonkotsu (pork bone broth) ramen of Kyushu to the miso ramen of Hokkaido. The basic ingredients of these noodles are wheat flour, eggs, salt, water, and kansui, which is essentially a type of alkaline mineral water, containing sodium carbonate and usually potassium carbonate, as well as sometimes a small amount of phosphoric acid.

Taishoken is an over 50 year-old well known Ramen noodle restaurant chain in the Tokyo area started by [133]Kazuo Yamagishi (1934 - 2015) in 1961. The noodle dish they provide is traditional

132 Wikipedia: Ramen. Online at http://en.wikipedia.org/wiki/Ramen_noodles
133 Wikipedia: Kazuo Yamagishi (山岸一雄). Online at http://en.wikipedia.org/wiki/Wagyu

Tokyo style ramen with soup with chicken and bonito dashi and "koikuchi" soy-sauce or miso. Toppings normally include "menma" (bamboo shoots), "chashu" (baked or steamed and thinly sliced pork), and spinach and sometimes half of a boiled egg. Noodles are made of flour, eggs kansui, which is essentially a type of alkaline mineral water containing sodium carbonate and usually potassium carbonate, and a small amount of phosphoric acid and the width is medium, neither too fat nor too thin. The Taishoken chain is great for many Tokyoites with average income or less because of the affordable price and extremely generous helpings.

Also, there is a different Ramen shop chain named Taishoken with a completely different taste of soup and culinary tradition from Yamagishi's Taishoken. Among those in the second chain, Taishoken in Eefukucho has the highest reputation and there is consistently a long lineup in front of the restaurant[134].

[135]Preparing Suppon (Soft-shell Turtle) Meal

134 永福町大勝軒. Online at http://eifuku-taishouken.com/
135 The picture is taken by the author, 2009.

[136]Japanese beef farmers who produce top quality meat called wagyū, known as Matsusaka beef (松阪牛) or Kobe beef (神戸牛), greatly respect the lives of beef cattle and treat them like family members. They are affectionate with these animals and treat them equally or better than their cats and dogs. They pamper them and feed them rice, other grains, sake or beer of premium quality, and regularly give them massages. They celebrate the day these cattles go to a slaughter house like a wedding feast. They send cows to the market just as they would send their daughters to their prospective husbands. They firmly believe that the transformation to the meal with highest quality is the happiest and most honorable moment for the cattle. These farmers often assign their children to feed and look after the precious cattle. This is very educational for children although they may feel sad momentarily. However, they learn the truth that they must take and eat lives of either animals or plants to survive by looking after cattle that the family has cherished dearly and sold for meat.

Some Japanese are also enjoy the challenge of extremely spicy curry that even most of the Indian or South Asian population are not able to consume. They often challenge each other to eat curry with 50 or 100 times larger quantity of chili pepper. For instance "gojukkara curry" (50辛カレー) contains 50 times more hot pepper than the standard curry and many people have tried to eat it as a competition. Spicy curry eating contests are one of many different kinds of food related competitions Japanese enjoy. They also compete for the maximum amount of food they can consume. They have sushi, soba or ramen eating contests and compete for a championship as if it were an athletic activity.

There is one more well known Tokyo Tower's event in which free food is provided to visitors. Tokyo Tower Sanma Festival is an annual event held every September, and 3,333 early visitors are provided

136 Wikipedia: Wagyu. (和牛). Online at http://en.wikipedia.org/wiki/Wagyu

free grilled Sanma or Pacific Saury. The pacific saury also known by the name mackerel pike is an autumn delicacy in some East Asian cuisines. The fish is called *sanma* (サンマ / 秋刀魚) in Japanese, *kongchi* (꽁치) in Korean, *qiu dao yu* (秋刀魚) in Chinese. The Kanji characters used in the Chinese and Japanese names of the species (秋刀魚) signifies "autumn knife fish", in reference to its configuration, somewhat resembling a knife, and its best season is fall.

The average overall body length of the fish is approximately 36 - 41 cm, and their maximum reported lifespan is two years. Sanma is one of the most prominent seasonal delicacies representing autumn in Japanese cuisine. It is most commonly served salted and grilled whole, with grated daikon radish, and condiments like soy sauce, or lime, lemon, or other citrus juices. In Tokyo Tower Sanma Festival, they serve free Saury as grilled whole garnished with grated daikon and a small citrus called Kabosu. Many people choose not to gut the fish although the intestines are bitter. They enjoy the bitterness, balanced by the condiments and daikon[137].

In Sanma Festival, they also sell Sanma burgers and Sanma miso soup at reasonable prices. Every year, they transport over 6,000 saury fish from Ofunato City in Iwate prefecture for the Tokyo Tower Sanma Festival. Ofunato was a fishing community badly damaged by the Tōhoku Earthquake in March 2011. After the earthquake hit Ofunato and destroyed the fishery businesses there, the community started utilizing Tokyo Tower Sanma Festival to let the public know that the fishery is recovering and to promote their businesses. A volunteer group from Ofunato City named Sanma Rangers[138] grill Saury with chacole *hibachi* and serve each visitor until first 3,333 fish run out.

---

137 Wikipedia: Pacific saury. Online at http://en.wikipedia.org/wiki/Pacific_saury
138 "Sanma Rangers" are apparently modeled after "Power Rangers", however they do not wear special uniforms.

Cities

Yokohama is a large city located by the beach in the outskirts of Tokyo. They have many high-rise hotels from which their patrons can view the spectacular skyline of downtown Tokyo including Tokyo Tower and Tokyo Skytree, a couple of well-known landmarks of the Japanese capital. The skyline of Tokyo downtown is even more spectacular after dusk because all high-rise buildings there have light-ups. I recommend you become a patron of high-rise hotels in Tokyo or her surroundings if you have a chance to travel there and your wallet gives you a permission to do it.

Shinkansen is very well-known bullet train in Japan with a good reputation for speed, safety and good service. Subways in the populated areas of major cities are networked like spider webs. People who live in big cities in Japan do not feel the necessity to drive cars on a daily basis because train systems are the best and most reliable part of the country. If you live in Japanese cities, you will find that the trains are the most convenient and trustworthy transportation, which keep you from the hassles and hazards of driving vehicles in heavy and dangerous traffic.

[139]Meiji Mura (博物館明治村) is a tourism-focused open-air architectural museum/theme park located in a suburban area of Nagoya. The museum moved over 60 historic buildings from Japan's Meiji (1867–1912), Taisho (1912–1926), and early Shōwa (1926–1989) periods. The most noteworthy building there is the reconstructed main entrance and lobby of the landmark Imperial Hotel designed by an American architect Frank Lloyd Wright (1867 – 1959), that originally stood in Tokyo from 1923 to 1967. If you are keen on Japanese history, architecture and arts, you will certainly enjoy this museum.

---

139 Wikipedia: Meiji Mura. Online at http://en.wikipedia.org/wiki/Meiji_Mura

[140]Roppongi Hills (六本木ヒルズ) is one of the new urban centres of Tokyo located in the Roppongi district. It is a mega-complex that incorporates office space, apartments, shops, restaurants, cafés, movie theaters, a museum, a hotel, a major TV studio, an outdoor amphitheater, and a few parks. Many tourists visit the top floors and the roof to see the spectacular panoramic views of the city. From there, visitors enjoy viewing landmarks such as Tokyo Tower, Tokyo Skytree, Rainbow Bridge, Tokyo Gate Bridge and the Imperial Palace. It is easy to fantasize a character like Spiderman jumping into Tokyo Tower or Skytree using a spider web coming out from their wrists. Perhaps a "reality check" would be important before going up to the top!

Surprisingly, some hotels in Tokyo and Yokohama have panorama restrooms with a huge glass window in front of a toilet and urinary. Perhaps they are designed to make travelers feel victorious by sitting on a toilet like a throne on the highest pinnacle of a mega city. But they obviously do make people very vulnerable to voyeurism.

Kabuki is one of the most well known theatrical arts started during the Edo period. The performance is the combination of singing and dancing and extremely long sessions which include full-day programs. Also, in the Kabuki theatre, all characters including females are played by male actors. The actors who play female characters are called 女形 (onna gata) and are trained to act like a women since childhood. Stories in Kabuki include legends, forklore and myths from different age periods[141].

Celebrations

Japanese typically celebrate New Year's at Shinto shrines and buy ceremonial items like the "New Years Arrow" and "omamori" (お守り) or a small accessory supposedly to protect a person from a bad luck

140 Wikipedia: Roppongi Hills. Online at http://en.wikipedia.org/wiki/Roppongi_ Hills
141 Wikipedia: Kabuki. Online at http://en.wikipedia.org/wiki/Kabuki

and evil spirits. They also celebrate the Fall Festival at Shinto shrines and young and old men carry a mobile sanctuary called "mikoshi" (神輿) around the city. At the end of the festival all men and women eat special food and drink plenty of sake because the Fall Festival is originally a celebration of the harvest. According to the tradition, these people are supposed to consume newly harvested food in the feast since Fall Festival has an origin in farming communities. In rural communities they still consume rice, vegetables and fruit just come from their farms, and meat from animals slaughtered right before the feast. The same festival is held in urban areas since almost all city centers and metropolitan districts were originally farming communities over centuries of years ago.

Bōnenkai is a Japanese drinking party that is held at the end of the year, generally among groups of co-workers or friends. The objective of the party, as the name indicates, is to forget the woes and griefs of the past year, and hopefully look to the New Year, usually by consumption of large amounts of alcohol. The behavior of some Bōnenkai participants are often inappropriate and excessive. Bōnenkai does not take place on any specific day, but they are usually held anytime during the month of December. This custom started in the 15th century during the Muromachi period (室町時代1337 to 1573) as 納会 (noukai) or achieved a great thing party. Later on, in the 18th century, a new word Bōnenkai or year-end party came into existence in various writings or historical documents[142].

Shinnenkai is held with the purpose of welcoming the arrival of the New Year. In North America, people celebrate mainly on New Year's Eve and the following the morning of New Years Day. However, people in Japan and some other Asian countries, celebrate the New Year during the entire month of January. Shinnenkai is a little more conservative in comparison with Bōnenkai. However, people still

142 Wikipedia: Bōnenkai. Online at http://en.wikipedia.org/wiki/B%C5%8Dnenkai

consume plenty of alcohol. In the same way as Bōnenkai, Shinnenkai is generally held among co-workers or friends anytime during January. In Shinnenkai people also consume rice cake made of sticky sweet rice and Osechi or traditional New Years food consisting of seafoods, meat and vegetables. In Shinnenkai there is more of an emphasis on food than alcohol while Bōnenkai has a heavier emphasis on drinking since the main objective is forgetting bad things during the entire year and alcohol helps you accomplish it[143].

For instance, there is no traditional meal for Bōnenkai, and people might consume all kinds of food served with alchohol. However, in Shinnenkai, people enjoy traditional Osechi and Zoni soup with omochi or sticky rice cake along with alchohol. Besides that, in Shinnenkai, people are required more discipline as they consume alcohol. The obnoxious and obscene behaviours are not permissible in the New Years party although some drink heavily as in Bōnenkai. Besides Shinnenkai, New Year's family celebrations take place usually during the first three days of a year. The breakfast during the first three days is most important for them. People usually consume sake with traditional New Year's Osechi meal with Zoni soup, but family celebrations are much more conservative than publicly held Shinnenkai.

Other seasonal festivities like equinox and solstice are usually celebrated in Buddhist temples instead of Shinto shrines. The most well-known seasonal festival celebrated in Buddhist temples would be "Setsubun" (節分)[144] known as Bean-Throwing Festival takes place the day before the beginning of spring, and many YouTubers upload their creations about it. They do a ceremonial Bean-Throwing ritual to kick out "Oni" (鬼) from their property and eat extremely long maki sushi called "Eho Maki" (恵方巻き) or symbolical food for a good life that they eat while facing the yearly lucky compass direction,

143 Wikipedia: Shinnenkai. Online at http://en.wikipedia.org/wiki/Shinnenkai
144 Wikipedia: Setsubun. Online at http://en.wikipedia.org/wiki/Setsubun

determined by Asian zodiac symbol of that year. In [145]Tokyo Tower, a communications and observation tower where many foreign tourists visit, there is an annual "Setsubun" (節分) celebration in which "Eho Maki" is served and all visitors can participate in the Bean-Throwing ceremony. The participants there eat "Eho Maki" while facing the yearly lucky compass direction from the main observatory of the steel tower. It is generally considered the celebration of the arrival of the spring and takes place almost simultaneously with Groundhog Day in the West.

Japanese urban legends (都市伝説)

[146] Japanese urban legends 都市伝説 (Toshi Densetsu) are enduring modern folktales in which preternatural creatures attack ordinary people or non-paranormal, and widespread rumors about them in popular culture. The former usually include 怨霊 (onryo), Japanese ghosts who have become vengeful spirits and take their aggression out on any who cross their path instead of the fantastical or animistic 妖怪 (yokai), or supernatural creatures of earlier Japanese folklore and myth. Modern urban legends tend to takes place in Japanese school properties and, similar to the yokai legends, often incorporate cautionary tales into their stories, warning people against problematic behaviors like bullying others, walking home late at night, urinating publicly or talking to strangers. There are also several non-supernatural urban legends in Japan's cities, such as the secret Tokyo tunnels built by the Imperial Japanese Army before the First World War or the corpse-washing job with extraordinary high wages. Japanese urban legends have a close parallel with Lafcadio Hearn's studies in the 19th century who did an in-depth study of Japanese culture, spirituality and the world of yokai and ghosts after immigrating to Japan from Britain[147].

145 Tokyo Tower (東京タワー). Online at http://www.tokyotower.co.jp/index.html
146 Wikipedia: Japanese urban legends. Online at http://en.wikipedia.org/wiki/Japanese_Urban_Legends
147 Wikipedia: Lafcadio Hearn. Online at http://en.wikipedia.org/wiki/Lafcadio_Hearn

[148]There is a very a powerful Tokyo based urban legend concerning a mediaeval age warlord named平将門 (Taira no Masakado). He was one of the most well-known historical figures in Tokyo, a samurai class warlord who fought as a rebel against the imperial court and the government in Kyoto in the 900s and attempted to start a new monarchy in the Kantō region that became today's Tokyo. He was eventually beheaded, and his head was transported to Kyoto and publicly displayed. However, according to the legend his head flew over from Kyoto to Tokyo and fell to the location that eventually became Tokyo. People in the village over there buried the head and built a Shinto shrine named [149]首塚 (Kubizuka) which literally meant "head shrine" to honor Masakado who fought against the corrupted court and government in Kyoto. After his death, Masakado became very popular figure among the peasant class in his own district.

The shrine that was built over his head is in the financial district in downtown Tokyo, and some Tokyoites believe that Masakado is a malevolent spirit who haunts the area around his shrine. The legend has grown over the years, as mysterious negative things have happened to those who have tried to move or demolish the shrine. Even today, the legend is very powerful and higher-ups in offices around the shrine come to pay their respects, and employees in nearby buildings refuse to sit with their backs to Masakado's head. Besides Kubizuka, Tokyoites built another Masakado Shinto shrine named神田明神 (Kanda-myōjin) which meant "god of enlightenment in Kanda"[150] or Kanda Shrine. Unlike Kubizuka, Kanda Shrine is an ordinary Shinto shrine, and there is no paranormal Toshi Densetsu concerning this.

148   Tokyo Travel Blog: Tokyo Urban Legends. http://www.nileguide.com/destination/blog/tokyo/2010/04/05/tokyo-urban-legends/
149   Wikepedia: 平将門の首塚. Online at http://ja.wikipedia.org/wiki/%E5%B9%B3%E5%B0%86%E9%96%80%E3%81%AE%E9%A6%96%E5%A1%9A
150   Wikepedia: Kanda Shrine. Online at http://en.wikipedia.org/wiki/Kanda_Shrine

Kubizuka and Kanda Shrine, during the centuries, played two ambivalent and opposing roles. For those in the court and central government, they existed for the sake of pacifying the angry ghost of Taïra-no-Masakado, a warlord who rebelled against the imperial court. However, for those outside of the government structure, particularly in the Tokyo area where his rebellion actually happened, these shrines are places to empower people to fight against corrupted leaders, since Masakado was a Kami who could liberate them from the oppression of rulers in any ages[151].

[152]The first story of a popular Japanese TV drama series titled 都市伝説の女 (Toshi Densetsu no Onna: 2012) is based on the legend that the ghost of Taira no Masakado attacks on the living. In this TV drama series, a young and sexy female police officer 音無月子 (Tsukiko Otonashi) works for the First Investigation Division team. Tsukiko is a typical Otaku generation young woman and dresses up like anime characters. She is also so obsessed with urban legends that she claims she became a detective because of "Toshi Densetsu". Whenever a case happens, she contemplates whether it may have any relations to "Toshi Densetsu".

[153]In The first day that Tsukiko takes up her post at the Tokyo Metropolitan Police Department, the dead body of Fujisawa Masafumi, an employee of Hagino Denko at Otemachi is found near Masakado's Kubizuka. Because Fujisawa has fallen to the ground and died, Tsukiko wonders "Maybe this case has something to do with Toshi Desetsu." However, her boss Ichio Tannai and and other colleagues are astonished by Tsukiko's remark and disregard it as an absurd comment. After that, Tannai comes to the conclusion that

151 Isao Ebihara. Land of Rising Ghosts & Goblins. (Dayton, TN: USA: Global Ed Advance Press, 2012)

152 AsianWiki: Toshi Densetsu no Onna. Online at http://asianwiki.com/Toshi_Densetsu_no_Onna

153 Asahi.co.jp: Toshi Densetsu no Onna. https://jdramas.wordpress.com/2012/04/13/toshi-densetsu-no-onna/

it is a suicide case and decides to close it because a suicide note is discovered at Fujisawa's home. However, Tsukiko does not believe that Fujisawa had any reason to take his own life. She continues to do her own investigation, disobeying Tannai's order, Tsukiko discovers that it was neither suicide nor Masakado's curse related incident, but a homicide case. Fujisawa was murdered by his boss Ryoichi Hagino since he was trying to expose his company's corruption. At the end of the story, Tsukiko remarked that she was glad that the spirit of Masakado guided her to the solution of the case although her primary assumption was wrong.

YouTube and Japanese Culture

Trains, cities, buildings and many different food items in Japan are also very popular and entertaining items for those creating YouTube videos. For many outsiders new to the country, these items are unique and fascinating. The "Shinkansen" bullet trains from outside and inside, since these trains are unique and engrossing items for those who live outside of the country. These videos include train stations and scenery in cities and country sides viewed from the windows. And the videos usually accompany brief illustrations about the locations that trains were passing and instructions about how to board the train. The process to obtain the boarding pass and pass the gate to the train is fully computerized and they use a fashionable system called "SUICA" with similar pronunciation as "suika" (西瓜) or watermelon. Viewers can also observe how typical train riders behave in these trains. Such new passenger controlling systems are also as intriguing as the trains per se for many techno geeks who come from the overseas. Some videos also introduce regular express trains slower than "shinkansen", much slower local trains, subways and commuter trains in city centres normally filled with people during the rushhour.

Numerous kinds of foods consumed in Japan are also a very fascinating part for YouTube viewers and makers. A tremendous number of foodie YouTubers, both Japanese nationals and non-Japanese, created videos dealing with culinary culture in Japan. Many of them might have been inspired to climb up the ladder to Internet celebrity status, since food is a universally popular topic and easiest to get public attention. The vast majority of non-Japanese YouTubers take videos of sushi, various kinds of noodles and "kaiseki" or meals typically served in "ryokan" or traditional Japanese style inns and traditional Japanese restaurants. Some like to focus on the western foods in Japan like "tonkatsu" (とんかつ) or pork cutlet, Japanese style pasta or "hanbaagu" (ハンバーグ) or hamburger steak. However, some of them are into more exotic food items like "fugu" (河豚) or blowfish, "suppon" (鼈) or soft-shell turtles and "unagi" or eels (鰻). Some YouTubers are fascinated with "osechi" (おせち) speciality foods for New Year or "ekiben" (駅弁) or "bento" lunch box sold in "eki" or train stations and consumed in trains while customers are traveling. YouTube producers often introduce typical Japanese homes and some distinct customs such as taking shoes off at a certain square shaped area with concrete or tile paved floor near the main enterance called "genkan" (玄関). Japanese typically use slippers at home and they usually wear separate pairs in their restrooms. YouTube makers display their "genkan", restrooms, kitchens and bedrooms with "tatami" mats. They also explain how to use their bathtubs and several different kinds of toilets there. In Japan, entire families share the same bath water, so that it must be kept clean until the last person takes a bath. People must take a shower and clean themselves outside of the bathtub. Some older homes have traditional toilets in which people must squat, but some other homes have Western style ones. Then, the most fascinating kind of toilets for YouTube viewers might be Western style in appearance but embedded with newer high-tech functions such as a water fountains or hot air that emits from them.

Producers also upload videos of various events including seasonal Buddhist or Shinto based festivities like the New Year's celebration, equinox, solstice and Fall Festival.

[154]Interior of Okonomiyaki Restaurant.

---

154 The picture is taken by the author, 2009.

Conclusion

In conclusion, I want to emphasize the Japanese language and culture as a part of the global heritage, not just a current fad or fascination. Just like any other cultural heritage, Japanese culture and language is a product of a unique anthropological, historical and religio-spiritual development over millenia. As globalization attains a mature stage, there are no more culturally isolated sovereign nations as the Galapagos Islands. The entire global community, however, operates as one living entity instead of a collection of individual organisms. Any nation-state separated from the global earth community will not be able to survive just as a living organ extracted from a human body.

From the late 20th century, Japanese culinary culture and the Otaku phenomena have had a large impact on the global community and will continue to impact human society indefinitely. The boundaries of sovereign nations are becoming continuously more ambiguous and Japan as a nation-state could cease to exist at some time in the future. However, Japanese food and anime cultures as global heritages may continue to play important roles in people's lives.

UNESCO added Japanese cuisine to the world heritage list in 2013. To my understanding, the enlistment of the Japanese culinary tradition to the world heritage list indicates that in this century, the Japanese food culture is a shared property which belongs to all human beings on this planet.

Likewise, Otaku or Anime/Manga culture, Japanese pop culture in a broader sense and more traditional high culture that originated in this island nation will be the heritage of the earth community accessible to the world's population. In my second book, "Shinto War Gods of Yasukuni Shrine", I discussed that how the term "culture will one day be divorced from ethnicity, nationality and sovereign states. Not only Japan, but all nation-states in a traditional sense, and their goverments, except for the developing world, have already lost control over their people and surrendered their social, economic and part of political power to the global community. It is a little more than 100 years after [155]Karl Marx predicted the death of the sovereign nations as the ultimate outcome of 19th Century capitalism.

Sovereign nations seem to be devolving into regional communities that look like independent prefectures or provinces under one global entity. Some of them still have a powerful appearance with a strong military like the United States or China. But they are powerless over global corporations or capitals, since militaries could not operate without the technologies created by the industries. In the 20th Century, industries are under the leash of governments. However, as Marx predicted in the next two centuries, almost all governments of individual states have lost control over the industries.

Thus, in the next phase of world order, various cultures could exist independently from ethnic origins and continue to evolve dynamically in the coming era if globalization moves into an advanced stage and all nation-states die out. Japanese culinary culture, anime/manga culture and pop culture in a broader sense and more traditional high culture will continue to evolve and transform as one of the vital sub-cultures of the whole human culture. For instance, sushi in the 24th century in StarTrek in other Sci-Fi world will be a product

---

155 Wikipedia: Karl Marx. Online at http://en.wikipedia.org/wiki/Karl_Marx

completely out of imaginations for those living in the 20th and 21st, while still following the tradition originated in the 18th century's Japan.

Unlike sovereign nations and their goverments which could die out after exercising the defacto power over people's lives during the previous few centuries, various languages on earth are likely to exist continuously as means of communication, being closely attached to constantly evolving cultures. As an effect of globalization, some of the unique characteristics of Japanese language and culture will be modified. The extreme "higher-context" nature of the language and culture will curved into more "lower-context" side, and the number of "keigo" 敬語 or "super-polite" expressions will be significantly reduced, although they will likely not be completely eliminated. However, the uniqueness and enigma of Japanese will be retained because of its origin, syntax and cultural formation. Since language and culture remain an inseparable symbiosis during the advanced stages of globalization, the Japanese language will continue to play a pivotal role to decode the enigma of the culture in the next few centuries.

In Chapter Four, I discussed people who have resided in Japan during significantly long periods and developed their careers successfully and reached C2 or the highest point of Can-do with equivalent or higher competency than the average Japanese native speaker. They are also well versed in the entertainment and pop culture as well as traditional high culture like history, politics and religions in Japan. They may be the true cosmopolitans and global citizens with multi-cultural competency.

With proper guidance from the ultimate higher power, these individuals are also good candidates to receive a title "world changer" after completing long journeys of life, since they have great potential to contribute to the global community by demonstrating unique inter-cultural perspectives and impetus to demolish national and cultural boundaries in an ultimate sense.

[156] Bleach Photo 2[157].

156 Was available June 2014: www.azhime.com
157 The picture is used under "fair dealing" (Canada) and "fair use" (USA) provisions in copyright law.

About the Author

Isao Ebihara, D.Phil. (Oxford Graduate School, TN), a native of Japan, has resided in Canada for over 25 years. He has taught Japanese language courses at Trinity Western University in British Colombia since 2002. His academic training encompasses theology, psychology and literature, and his interests include Japanese language, Asian animation and pop culture, culture and spirituality and religions and politics. Dr. Ebihara has a thorough knowledge of Japanese anime culture and recognizes its great impact on the global community.

In his 2010 book, *All the World is Anime: Religions, Myths & Spiritual Metaphors in the World of Japanimation & Manga*, he explored the philosophical and religious/spiritual background of the anime authors and stories and a history of their productions.

In his 2011 book, *Shinto War Gods of Yasukuni Shrine: The Gates of Hades and Japan's Emperor Cult*, Dr. Ebihara made a comparison of the cultural and historical components of Shinto religion to pop cultures including anime (Japanese animations) and manga (Japanese comics), drawing upon the work of Alan J.P. Taylor's populist or "anti-great man" approach and Carl Jung's archetype theory.

In his 2012 book, *Land of Rising Ghosts & Goblins: The supernatural world in Japanese Myths, Folklores, Anime & Pop-Culture*, Dr. Ebihara examined the world of ghosts, spirits, supernatural phenomena and incidents in Japanese mythology, folklore and legends from antiquity to novels and today's modern tales of anime and manga.

    This book was written out of a realization that students need something more than a textbook when studying a foreign language. It includes various levels of the Japanese language/culture to be utilized by students to review their learning and may also be a handbook for the Japanese culture as well as the language. It combines chapters of plain introduction of Japanese grammar and discussions of cultural components including culinary and pop culture together.

Lightning Source UK Ltd.
Milton Keynes UK
UKOW07f2158290515

252587UK00001B/1/P